What people are saying about *IHood: Our GPS for Living*

"*IHood: Our GPS for Living* is a thought inspiring book that provides a compass for those of us navigating the waters of life."

– Jack Luchsinger, Attorney and Author,
The Thirteenth Disciple- Soldier or Saint.

"If you've ever had an ego problem through false pride, where you think more of yourself than you should or through fear or self-doubt when you think less of yourself than you should, you need to read *IHood: Our GPS for Living*. Read this book and learn how to get out of your own way."

– Ken Blanchard, Co-Author, *The One Minute Manager* and *Lead Like Jesus*

"*IHood* is an uplifting and inspiring work written by a born teacher, and a born evangelist. She lived her life with a sense of great and noble purpose, and she served her students with wise love and loving wisdom. That sense of purpose is evident on every page, as is her great, transforming sense of wonder. Therefore, I would recommend it to all who are looking for comfort and inspiration in their lives."

– Joseph M. McShane, S.J., President, Fordham University

"*IHood* takes you on a journey of self-reflection which I deeply believe will naturally make you a better person for it gently moves you towards being a beacon of your own destiny. Once you read this book, you will be inspired to live every day, more fully, more brightly and more generously with those you know and those whom you may come to know, with love".

– Lanette Ware-Bushfield, Actress/Writer and
Executive Producer, a Bushfield Production, Inc.

"This book will change lives, you have so much tenacity and spiritual connection to the Divine, that this book will be embraced by the masses."

– Bonita Shear, Women's Empowerment Coach
and National Speaker on Women's Health

"Dr. Little presents a compelling discussion of faith as the essence of personal direction."

– Lee A. Black, Insurance Executive

"What a great teaching resource guide for specific growth periods, discussion groups for so many age groups and the teachers that must connect with their students. So much potential to have a syllabus accompany this book."

– Rosalind Schwartz, Retired Teacher

"This book could be proverbial light at the end of the legendary tunnel for many, especially new and confused parents."

– Dr. Barry Quinn

"An inspirational read with practical tips that we can incorporate in our own lives. The reader is guided on a journey; a GPS system to help us find our way home or back to living an authentic life. This book is divinely inspired."

– Laura's List: Books for Women

"Dr. Jill Little has taken a quantum leap forward in systematically delineating the true purpose of life and more importantly, how to recognize it and even more importantly, how to achieve it. Humanity needs this book."

– Richard Hassan, Entrepreneur

"I loved Jill's insight into how we can all get along better in this world and her ideas for how to improve our journey. I'm so happy she finished the book before leaving the earth plane. I know this book will help so many people."

– Elizabeth Wright, Author of *I & Eye: A Guide to Vibrational Healing & My Transformation Journey to the Light*

"As a former 7th grade teacher, I've always felt that the classroom lessons on treating each other well were more important than the academic subject. Jill's book supports that theory."

– Kathie Vasell

"I really enjoyed the two big takeaways from the first part of the book: the need to keep God and spirituality in your life and the critical role parents play in the early development of the child."

– Que Spaulding, Retired Executive

"I have been fortunate enough to call Jill Little a friend. She has defined and revealed moments in life which affect and guide us. 'Only those who can see the invisible can do the impossible.' This book demonstrates this and is a testament to these words as well as to a life well lived."

– Laurie Adams Warren

"I know I will find myself referring back to IHood many times in the coming years. Thank you for presenting a book that truly makes sense and making the reader a better person."

– Eloise Luchsinger, Skaneateles Furs

"I loved the book. Life is so chaotic and it's very easy to get completely lost in the everyday craziness. This book is a great "gps" to guide you back on the right path."

– Lynne Sweet, Manager of Skaneateles Country Club

"All ages can be inspired by this book to gain valuable knowledge to comfort and guide them throughout their personal journeys."
– Suzanne Congel

"Loved the book, especially the personal stories and examples."
– Kimberly Forbes

"An excellent book propelling self discovery. Would benefit an audience of 15-30 year olds to read alongside a parent; great discussion book."
– Janella

"Jill's personal revelation, writings and interpretation of famous sociologists and psychiatrists, and her urgency to share this message with the world brings forth peace, love and truth."
– Bonnie Romano

"Jill's book is very revealing and makes the reader truly look deep inside one's self to better understand our duty, job and commitment while we are here. It takes us on a journey of life and forces us to reconcile what our life is in its current state and what it could be. Some books come along that helps to put our lives into perspective, this is one of them."
–Maureen Famiano/ Executive Producer
Riverbank Studios- WFLA Television Tampa

IHood:
Our GPS for Living

Jill Little PhD

WESTBOW
PRESS
A DIVISION OF THOMAS NELSON

WestBow Press books may be ordered through booksellers or by contacting:

WestBow Press
A Division of Thomas Nelson
1663 Liberty Drive
Bloomington, IN 47403
www.westbowpress.com
1-(866) 928-1240

Because of the dynamic nature of the Internet, any web addresses or links contained in this book may have changed since publication and may no longer be valid. The views expressed in this work are solely those of the author and do not necessarily reflect the views of the publisher, and the publisher hereby disclaims any responsibility for them.

Any people depicted in stock imagery provided by Thinkstock are models, and such images are being used for illustrative purposes only.

Certain stock imagery © Thinkstock.

ISBN: 978-1-4497-8308-2 (sc)
ISBN: 978-1-4497-8309-9 (hc)
ISBN: 978-1-4497-8307-5 (e)

Library of Congress Control Number: 2013901574

Printed in the United States of America

WestBow Press rev. date: 3/11/2013

Dedication

This book is dedicated to those who made it possible for me to express myself through writing. I am especially grateful to my husband and family who had the patience to assist me in whatever tasks developed, as I devoted nearly two years to writing *IHood: Our GPS for Living*. I would foremost like to thank God who regularly awakened me at night with new revelations now contained in this book. As a result of God's inspiration, my guiding philosophy in life is "Help people who need love so they overcome challenges and find their life's purpose."

Be an instrument of love.
- Jill Little

Table of Contents

Acknowledgment

IHood: Our GPS for Living was published and distributed with the help of many people. I am certain Jill would like to thank Laura Ponticello for her fine job in marketing and coordinating the efforts that saw *IHood: Our GPS for Living* through to its final form. We were blessed to have had the exceptional graphic talents of Cynthia Prado. Karen Wallingford provided outstanding creative writing and editing, and the development of our web presence. The myriad of administrative functions were exceptionally fulfilled by Janelle Kite. The work of these women has made publishing Jill's book a pleasant experience, and I feel blessed to be spreading the message she was so passionate about.

I would also like to thank all those who worked with me behind the scenes and contributed to what has become Jill's lasting legacy.

Thank you all for your efforts.

Sincerely,
Edward S. Little –husband to the late Dr. Jill Little

Foreword

Jill led by example. She was a natural teacher, philosopher, and student every day of her life; passionate in defining her purpose and helping others define theirs. She wrote this book in hopes of spreading the message of a purpose driven life and how to attain it, believing a sense of belonging in the world depended on it. Often she lay awake at night, scribbling notes of ideas and images that would flood her head and keep her awake. Her "downloads," as she called them, were occasionally ill timed and we later found notes on scraps of paper from hurried moments.

Jill focused on serving as an instrument of love and peace wherever she went. She made fast friends among casual encounters. She was a sympathetic ear and a compassionate soul who actively served to share her insights on life, love, and spirituality. She pursued a PhD in education, and her teaching career was further enhanced by a hunger to discover the path to her higher self through self-awareness and living a purposeful life. She has always been an inspiration to those who love her, and to have known her is to love her. This book is a testament to her wisdom, devotion to helping others, and generosity of spirit.

The messaging and distribution of this book consumed Jill's mind, body, and soul until a brain aneurysm interrupted her furious progress. Derailed by the aneurysm in October 2011, the book nearly finished, she spent the next five months hospitalized until her untimely death. For those five months, she continued to live the life she wanted, embracing the idea of heaven and its patient invitation as much as she embraced promising milestones that kept her with us a short while longer. Despite limited mobility and motor skills, she continued living her passion by becoming a more conscious human being. She started to share her awareness of the "other side." She was unafraid of the transition, and I was more connected to her in the last few weeks of her life than I had ever been.

In dying, she found purpose, just as she had in living. Jill left behind her greatest work, *IHood: Our GPS for Living* to share with all humanity.

- Jill's daughter, Dee

Note to the Reader

Dear friends:

Thank you for being part of a divine revolution. When I was given the message of *IHood*, I had no idea if He meant "Eyehood," like the middle eye of Eastern philosophy, or "IHood." Several writing sessions were needed before I was guided into the wisdom of understanding this brand new concept. I know the message is provocative, urgent, and intended to enlighten those who read and hear it. I am grateful for the educational training and experiences I've had, for they have prepared me for the awesome task of writing this book. *IHood: Our GPS for Living* has also made clear my purpose: to teach using God's words of wisdom and to heal my fellow travelers with those words, to be His instrument of love.

IHood will help you understand your personal journey on earth. It will give you the opportunity to reflect back upon your youth and social development by taking you through your stages of growing up, your personal maturation. This process will illuminate where you may have encountered difficulties, and help explain why you may have shortcomings in evolving to a higher level of motivation and maturation. It also will shed light on what motivates you and why.

In *I Am*, a documentary by film producer Tom Shadyac (*Ace Ventura, Bruce Almighty, Liar Liar*), I found a profound message of hope and love for our world; it is a sister message to that which is revealed in this book. After viewing this film, I was positive this book is meant to be part of a movement that will awaken those who are unconscious in our world. They will recognize that our purpose is to serve others and realize that in doing so, we are infinitely connected to each other in this world. The reward is deep contentment. Stress inhibits our brains, and anger makes us lose rationale. We function better in a state of love, as proven and measured in magnetic field studies. All living things on earth are entwined particles. We are not meant to be separate. We suffer when we see the suffering of others. It is in our DNA. This book encourages us to embrace this DNA and all living things while acknowledging that we are part of the whole earth; we are here, with purpose, to better our world.

You will notice at the end of each chapter, there are intricately designed blank pages for penning thoughts and reflections. This is space to ponder inspirations that come to you throughout each chapter, and to document them for future reference. Books that have helped me most during life's journey are those that inspire and foster deeper reflection of my own circumstance. As such, this space is intended as a place for you to pen thoughts, ideas, or reflections stimulated by *IHood: Our GPS for Living*.

Journaling is a powerful tool for tapping into our IHood. It is mindful and authentic self-reflection documented for later reference. When you write down your thoughts, your transformative process is remembered for its integral role in our maturation.

I encourage you to choose whatever lessons you glean from this book and adapt them to your own circumstances. In sharing my own philosophies and experiences, I hope you will find yourself filling up with incredible love, and sharing it with the world around you. Please share your ideas on spreading love and honoring those in your life at www.ihoodbook.com.

Lovingly,
Dr. Jill Little

The Symbolism of the Dragonfly

In my family room, where stacks of papers laid with original ideas for this book, is a lamp with a dragonfly. I turned on this writing lamp many times, inspired by the dragonfly. Dragonflies are symbolic of transformation. They go through many phases of change during their life cycles, and it is only after full maturation that their colors reach their full vibrancy.

A dragonfly adapts to the light around it, constantly metamorphosing in a variety of ways, much like the maturation process illustrated in *IHood: Our GPS for Living*. Throughout our life stages, we develop a stronger connection with our spiritual side, evoking light. We are able to recognize and control our egos, living more authentically and in service to others. Like colors on a dragonfly that emerge over time, so does our spiritual side. We have the power to transform, adapt, and ultimately display our true colors.

Dragonflies appeared in many examples as a symbol for this book. I knew with certainty that the dragonfly nestled on my writing lamp was not only symbolic of my own transformation as I wrote the book, but for the reader as well.

1
Our Purpose

We are born. We live. We die.

CYNICS HAVE MADE THIS simplistic observation about the human life story. If it were as basic as that, we would be like every animal on the planet. However, we are humans. Our species is unique. Many philosophers have what seems to be an eternal discussion on why we are here. Some believe we are here for the acquisition of material worth, that we exist solely for the pleasures of our physical world, trying to keep those needs satisfied.

Others of a different view feel the answer to this eternal question is more spiritual. Jesus actually gave the answer to why we are here when he said, "I am that I am." We are created because we have a purpose and are fully equipped to perform and complete that purpose when we enter this world. Our challenge is to awaken to this purpose and fulfill the challenges of living our life accordingly. It requires all of our physical and mental abilities, emotional stamina from our failures and triumphant experiences, and of course, love.

Unfortunately, we don't come into this life with a set of plans. We often have difficulty in discovering our purpose. We can wander through life committed to whatever demand a particular situation asks of us, and then move on to the next thing that requires our attention, unaware of a "grander" expectation. How many times do we hear "I'm doing the best I can"? Day to day life can be tedious and brimming with turmoil, precluding us from the ability to see our purpose clearly and routinely.

We all have our stories. Some tales are wrought with incredible pain and suffering: praying to survive extreme conditions, perhaps struggling daily just to find food and shelter. Then there are the "others" who seem to slide along without a care in the world, appearing to have everything they need—physically, emotionally and spiritually.

My story was of the survivor. Incredibly, I was born to a loving family, the youngest of three children. We weren't in a third world country; we were right here in good ol' USA. My parents had no advanced education; in fact they didn't continue beyond junior high school. There were good reasons in both cases; Dad's parents were both deceased by the time he turned thirteen, and Mom's dad died, forcing her to return from being boarded in a nearby rural town to take care of her younger three brothers so Grandma could work.

Though we faced financial challenges, we never accepted welfare. Dad had a lot of pride. Mom and Dad both worked to feed us, and still we were hungry more often than I can remember. I know my parents suffered.

After at least three moves that my young mind remembers, we moved to Grandma's. It was after World War II ended, and I had just turned five. That's when I started school. I was thrilled to be with my siblings in the same one room schoolhouse. The walk in deep snow was tough during winter, and my older sister had the added burden of sometimes pulling me on a sled. Our teacher,

Rachel Bisbo, was a family friend. She had eight grade levels to teach. It wasn't surprising the oldest students received the most attention as they had the more demanding curriculum. I would watch the presentations on the blackboard when I got bored and felt I should be doing more.

In spite of all the difficulties, I loved that year at Grandma's. We always had food. I learned how to fish, just like my sister and brother had, so that we would have supper. We also acquired the skills to make lye soap, prime the pump for drinking water, and take out the chamber pot, which was always positioned under Grandma's bed, to be used during the night. We learned to stack wood to prevent logs from falling on us if we grabbed more than one. Though there was no central heating, the wood stove in the kitchen was a miracle. We'd lay our clothes out before bed so we could make a run for it down the stairs and into the back of the house where we found reprieve from the frigid air in the only warm room. Meanwhile, the scent of cooked oatmeal made for breakfast made it all worth it.

When we left Grandma's house, I was scared again. I was only six, but I completely understood responsibility and survival. We used our two mattresses for living room furniture during the day and as beds at night. We were happy to have indoor plumbing. I learned that a little mustard on a piece of bread tasted pretty good, but not as good as Grandma's food. I couldn't wait until Grandma came for Christmas because I knew she would make bread, rolls, and pies, and we would eat like kings again.

Dad was a janitor for the apartment building we lived in, so I knew that as long as he kept this job, we would have a place to live. I learned how to take trash buckets to the curb and open the coal furnace so he could shovel coal into the huge cavern inside. He worked so hard, yet still we were so thin.

In school, I caught up with the children in first grade once my aunt taught me how to read. Luckily I enjoyed learning because my mother would say at least once a day, "Jill, you must get your education. Nobody can take an education away from you." I never knew who "nobody" was, but I understood my mother and her wisdom. Education was my ticket out of hunger and running from the landlord. At this point, I started paying close attention to my talents and skills. I also understood that there was definitely more to this life than survival.

When I was seven years old, I was stricken with bacterial meningitis. After my hospitalization, I spent many months in bed, leaving our basement apartment only to go to Dr. Wyatt's office for what Mom called "cold" shots, but I think they were vitamins. I'll never know. I just remember Dr. Wyatt's warm, Southern accent and the way he called me his sweetie pie.

It didn't take a rocket scientist to know all of the medical bills were taking a toll on my parents. I could hear the low voices at night. I remember feeling awful because I knew I was an "accident." Though I was unsure what it meant, I felt badly that I was creating added financial strain. I knew my parents loved me very much, but when I heard I was an "accident," even with laughter, I felt I had better earn my way and make people proud, because life perhaps, could have been easier without me.

It wasn't until I was in my fifties that I recognized how my entire life had been spent making sure I was a good person worthy of an accidental birth. Perhaps it explains the gradual transformation that began take over. After my illness, I began to think about a golden cross. It was larger than life, and it actually glowed when I closed my eyes and thought about God. It was so comforting. My family wasn't religious, but I began to hunger for it.

After Dad and Mom left the apartment house, we moved to

a rental not far from a Presbyterian Church. I begged to go, and Mom registered all three of us in Sunday school. I got my first Bible. It was red with gold on the edges. It was the prettiest gift I had ever received. I studied it, carrying it each Sunday to church to hear more about Jesus. Then we moved again.

We lived under Inez's flat from fifth grade through my high school graduation. It was amazing. I was never happier having friends and the ability to establish relationships was incredible. Neighbors would kindly take me to church with them; I tried every sect of the Protestant faith. It was not until after college that I became a Roman Catholic. I have my husband to thank for introducing me to my faith. I loved the humility and peaceful presence of the light that I felt, almost from the first time I attended mass. It was said in Latin, so I had no idea what was going on, but I knew beyond a doubt, it was where I belonged. I never told my mom about my conversion until after we married because she almost refused to attend my sister's wedding for the same reason. She had few nice words for Catholics, perhaps out of allegiance to the Methodist church where Grandma played the organ and where I was baptized when I was seven. It's sad that Mom never realized that the English versions of both churches are almost identical.

I believe I made my parents very proud. I wish they could have lived long enough to see me get my Ph.D., but I think graduating from college and becoming a teacher made them smile enough. They loved it too, when my children were born and we lived near them. It was a shock when my father died. I was eight months pregnant with our third child. I stayed during the day with him because his heart was beginning to fail, and Mom couldn't leave him alone while she worked. I will never forget the last day I was with him. I took some ironing with me and Dad played with my children, Bill and Dee in the living room. I rested for a bit following a slight fall I took that morning. When I left, it was the usual flurry of gathering the kids and fighting the weather to get to the car. Dad was at the dining room table and blew me a kiss. I waved hurriedly and scrambled out the door. I never said, "I love you" when I left. It wasn't on my mind. He died that night in the emergency room. I never said, "I love you."

Life goes on, but memories stay. The experiences mold us. We build ourselves from the potential we are given at birth. We become who we are because of God given gifts, and because of the circumstances in which we live. If we are lucky, during our maturation, we will recognize our inner voice that will mediate between our spirituality and our earth acquired ego. The recognition may not be as dramatic as the burning bush that spoke to Moses, directing him to lead the Israelites out of Egyptian slavery; in fact it may be as seemingly inconsequential as the moment when Moses first had his test of character. He was a grown man of privilege, living in Egypt when he witnessed an Egyptian beating a Hebrew and chose his own fate when he aligned with the powerless over the powerful. He murdered the overseer of the Hebrew and escaped to the desert after the pharaoh issued his death warrant. It was a life defining moment.

In the desert area of Midian, Moses married a shepherdess, Zipporah, and fathered a son, Gershom. It was during this time, as an elderly man, that he was called to lead his people from slavery. Of course, God was fairly explicit about His expectations, but Moses made a choice. It wasn't easy to accept this role. He was old and he was established in his community. He wasn't happy about being asked to fulfill this purpose. He begged God to make someone else his agent. We know God does not relent, he performed a series of miracles and Moses acquiesced, accepting his destiny and covenant with God; it was his purpose.

The continued story of Moses includes the gathering of the Ten Commandments. Though there was great drama and disappointment between Moses and his people, the outcome was an incredible covenant with the people. Our founding fathers, elaborating on the Moses narrative of being built on two pillars, glorified this covenant. The first, freedom, is when God liberates us from oppression, slavery, or pain, just as he freed the Israelites. The second is responsibility. There is an agreement between God and his people that we are to perform or refrain from certain activities, as He dictated in the Ten Commandments and there is no freedom without obligation.

So what does this all mean? Simply, that the light guides us into this world. We are given the freedom of choice to exist under certain conditions provided to us at birth. We are given gifts of skills and abilities, as well as the abiding spirit that keeps watch over our earthly existence from the moment we enter life, until we leave. In exchange, we are asked to develop our skills and talents to apply them in a purpose driven life that will help in creating a civil and just world.

We complete a human puzzle by developing and assessing our talents and abilities, and find space on this planet in which to plant them for posterity. When we finish our earthly task, which could take years or days or just a moment to complete (we don't know), we fill a space that was otherwise empty, leaving the world in a better, more complete state than when we entered it. We will have used all the loving care divined to us, and passed it onto people throughout our lives. What a perfect dream.

Reader Reflections

2
What is IHood?

Traveling Between Ego and Spirit

IHOOD IS OUR POWER center and GPS for living. It is not an organ that we can touch; it is a dynamic, invisible energy launched at the moment of birth. It is the home of our divine electrical charge; referencing our past for use as a touchstone for present and future decisions until it ceases at our death.

Just as we have an assigned identity to roles we play in life (motherhood, fatherhood, etc.), we have assigned individuality in our IHood. Our decisions and our interactions, originate in IHood. It is where we gain perspective and reflect on how an outside event affects us. Consequently, it becomes the birthplace of personal development and remains a commitment to who we are and how we relate to those around us. IHood is the dwelling place of the ego, the Holy Spirit, and our free will: the three ingredients necessary for survival and evolution.

One's IHood is directly affected by maturity. A child's choices are usually self-serving because children are motivated predominantly by ego. A child thinks: "if I want to eat more candy, I should be able to have more candy, because it tastes good." A more mature adolescent or adult might have a responsible thought process that is less ego driven such as, "I'm not going to eat all this candy! It's full of sugar, bad for my teeth, and will probably make me hyper. It's not worth it." By personally acknowledging the consequences of actions, it is easier to use restraint against the short lived, immediate satisfaction of candy. There tends to be a "me first" mentality as a child; a more redemptive, thee-first mentality (in this case, the long term care of our bodies) is the choice made following a period of maturation. Ego dominates the decision of free will in the first case; spirituality dominates in the second.

It isn't surprising that ego gets a stronghold on us in infancy/ childhood. We think we are the center of the universe. There is no recognition of the "other" except that the "other" meets our needs and demands. We are totally dependent. We could not survive without others, yet don't realize it. Parents are at a baby's beck and call, with no accolades for their servitude. Babies learn to cry as an alarm for attention; it's their signal for need satisfaction. Although needs change, the attitude of entitlement continues into the preadolescent years. Since pre-teens and teenagers are still children (albeit older), they require protection and security as well. They take for granted that adults will administer to them, unless unfortunate experiences occur where they have learned otherwise (parental neglect or unusual circumstance). They expect their hunger to be satisfied, a warm bed to sleep in, and arms to comfort them when life frightens them. Their ego develops dominance within IHood (their identity) because of repeated experiences of ego satisfaction necessary to a child's survival.

As a child progresses through the basic need filled years, parents are obliged to help their child to see that he or she is not the most important person in this world. This requires a loving approach because it is a startling revelation when parental behaviors start to shift from "You're the little king (queen)" to "It's time to be a team player!" Usually parents start with the basics, like please and thank you. Though this seems rudimentary, it must not be overlooked during a child's maturation. A good way of demonstrating appreciation is to spend time teaching children to send notes of gratitude to grandparents and friends who give gifts on special occasions. Children make a connection, they see that others are deserving of acknowledgment, and also see the appreciation of their acknowledgments, which makes them feel good. Eventually, he/she will behave voluntarily; perhaps as witnessed through thankful expressions to parents for giving them care. Parents may feel they will never see this day, but with proper guidance, children will ascend to this maturity and responsibility.

Without expectation of maturity and responsibility, children will feel entitled to be the center of the universe much too long. It depends on not only maturity, but on how motivated children are to become more independent. If parents have been particularly doting or the children have no obligations or expectations as contributing family members, the false notion of self-importance may perpetuate, and spirituality may be stalled. This has very negative consequences, since society has little tolerance for self-absorbed behavior. Parents are doing their children no favors by giving them a false sense of importance.

Once children begin to recognize the "feel good" outcome of appreciation from others, the effect of behaving in a more mature way and helping others will become more important to them. The children's spirituality, then, will become more important in their decision making. Egoic desire will be weighed more heavily against the experiences they rack up with the "helpful" or spiritual ones. They will begin to give more thought before making decisions about what they should or shouldn't do.

Ego has been the dominant force and has served children well thus far. However, less ego centric decisions will be direct choices when maturity is achieved. Self-serving decisions will be the first choices initially considered; however, children will make choices orchestrated by free will. This is how IHood operates. As we accumulate positive outcomes from decisions (our experiences), they will form the directions we will choose in our lifetimes. This is why maturity and motivation are keys to our development. We will constantly change our domination of ego, but it is a life challenge and the reason we call ourselves human.

IHood is a concept that is faith driven. It is composed of three essentials for our survival here on earth and for spiritual survival beyond our bodies: it is the embodiment of Holy Spirit, human ego, and free will. God, in his vision, recognized that we needed a human body in order to fulfill our spiritual mission. The combination of these two seemingly opposite aspects of life is interesting for one's IHood. Our existence is both world bound and spirit bound. We are undivided, yet we serve two masters: self and other. Ego is not seen as a negative element; rather an unconscious, me-oriented, need-driven part of our whole. Because of its importance during our early development, we are inclined to fall into its grasp; particularly when we feel under recognized or needy.

Our spirit, gifted at birth, is the truth of who we aspire to be and counters our self-centeredness; it leads us to our divine purpose. Our spirit guides us in the accomplishment of our human potential; a promise we keep to God to fulfill this unique purpose while in this world.

We are aware of our spirituality when it first stirs within our human body. We may see it through emotionality, when we identify with another who is in pain: we actually feel it; we internalize what they are experiencing. Perhaps this is why the audience cries out during film clips from funny home videos television shows when someone falls off a bike, crashes end over end, or when a dog takes a tumble. We get a measurable, physical reaction linking us with other earthly creatures. This is also why, on 9/11, there was a measurable energy that was picked up by instruments in our atmosphere right after the planes hit the towers. It was the compassion emoted by millions of people at once, a phenomenon never seen before or since.

Maturity and motivation also play major roles in each of us, as we become the best we can be. This treasure chest will be needed for our life's purpose. Developing and using the skills is our responsibility. We know innately that we need to do this; our parents spearhead the effort of this transformation as we work our way through school. Though we may be under the impression that the sole purpose of acquiring expertise is to make money, it is also our opportunity to help our fellow man.

As we mature, we recognize that we begin to build a value system. We value our collection of stamps, our ability to throw a ball, the money we receive that enables us to buy a new toy, our friends. The role of parents is extremely important in helping us sort out the hierarchy of what we value, as well as understand the larger system that operates throughout mankind. Parents may in fact have prejudices or biases that they unwittingly pass to their children in the process. Hopefully education and maturity can be tapped to eradicate false truths.

I remember as a second grader, bringing my friend home to play. My excitement was over the top, since I had never been allowed to do that, even though we lived next to the school. After my friend left, my dad told me I wasn't allowed to bring her home again. I remember crying in outrage. We had played ball against our large apartment house where my Dad was the janitor. We didn't create any mess and had behaved exemplarily, in my view. Dad simply said she wasn't our kind. That was it.

Many tears later, I begged my mom to explain what we had done. All she said was, "She's the wrong color." It never occurred to me that she was different from me. We laughed at the same things; we played the same games. The next day, I took a good look at my friend. She was a different color, but I decided it didn't matter to me. And I decided it never would matter to me. I figured my parents had never met somebody of another color that they could like. It was as simple as that. I was allowed to go to her house to play sometimes, and that was good enough for me.

I'm glad I was not influenced to believe as my parents believed. Children usually see and hear parental behavior and they mimic and respond in kind. They also grow to have values that support their own beliefs, dependent upon the outcome of certain experiences that occur. We will more than likely continue with beliefs that are positively reinforced. If a negative experience occurs, a re-evaluation will take place.

One area of value that seems to permeate the globe is the high value we place on the importance of having money. This is not surprising, since it is our barter for food, clothing, and shelter, among other things. In the United States, however, there seems to be an incredible offspring of value for "stuff," period. The more one has, the higher the esteem assigned to the owner. Big cars, big houses, fancy jewelry all drive our culture. This makes a shift from egoic behavior very challenging. We have an extremely high regard for monetary success, the fodder of our economy, the goal our parents place before us to emulate. Hollywood and sports figures exemplify this greed that feeds us. Materialism infiltrates our existence. It is no wonder children are motivated, above and beyond anything else, to make more money than they need. This is our success myth.

Is this bad? Are we so awful to desire houses and cars and comfort? Isn't this the American dream we are chasing? The stress to achieve a moneyed status presses to the point of cheating to get into the "right" college. Why do we exchange one value for another? How has money become the higher value?

One asks, is it bad to make money? Of course it isn't. It is only when we become compulsive and center our existence on the accumulation of wealth above all else that our values are exchanged for the "almighty dollar." Our full attention is toward acquisition of things. When this mindset dominates our behavior, it is driven by ego.

It is interesting to observe that nothing in nature takes more than it needs, except humans. Indigenous people call those who collect more than they need "crazy." They feel it is an illness, and perhaps it is. A misconception exists that more is better or more will make us happier. Tom Shadyac is a testimony to that in his film *I Am*[1]. I can also testify that, though my husband and I spent a lifetime accumulating households, furniture, and other stuff we thought were essential to our existence, at this point in my life, they aren't of value to me. We are selling what we don't need. I have sufficiently matured, and I understand that my time is best spent with my family and writing. My family was always the most important part of my life, but now I see the folly in "stuff"; belongings make people spend enormous amounts of time caring for possessions.

---

1   2011, Flying Eye Productions

If we are lucky, we will have parents who influence our movement from worldly satisfaction to enlightenment. This is when we can live without expectation, trusting that God has a plan for us. He has our best interests at heart since we are His creation. We can begin to focus on our living world which is, after all, our reason for being. The shift from being totally addicted to materialism frees the spiritual within us to evolve; it evokes IHood to pay more attention to the "other."

The ability to transform to a more meaningful life usually occurs sometime before young adulthood. It is a slow process, but social interaction begins to benefit from the gradual recognition of loving others, and positive outcomes begin to occur from enlightened behaviors. This awakening is critical, since never having the awareness of spirit imprisons us entirely within a bodily based, fear filled state of mind, leading to continued chaotic thought, full of apathy, depression, and other negativity. This egoic domination is the major reason for never finding peace and purpose. We never understand why we are here on this earth.

Influence of Maturation

Our life skills define us. As we mature, we explore who we are. Each level of maturation and physical development influences our ego and spirit. These include birth through two years, three through nine years; adolescence and puberty, adulthood and middle age, and advanced age. Maturation is a requirement for us to assimilate, change, and evolve.

The world that we live in is our creation. We may completely identify through pure ego satisfaction or with full cognition of our spirit, or both. We dig for new understanding of who we are as we awaken to our truth. It is important not to become impatient in the process. As we all have different DNA, quirky habits, different appearances, we all have different schedules to attain maturity. Each success we attain allows for more boldness in our attempt to awaken and live in spirit. The ego won't lead IHood to spirituality, but the loving guidance of our family and friends, and our spirit, will.

IHood is constantly looking to find its natural state of mind, adjusting and attempting to maintain its equilibrium. The ego keeps us fearful. It keeps us afraid that we won't get what we want, afraid that we won't belong, afraid that we aren't enough, afraid someone has more than we do; and on and on it goes. The ego is not sane. It is irrational. It becomes unconscious. We suffer in its arrogance; it cries out in need. It is the bane of our existence. Spirit, on the other hand, keeps our mind in peace, joy, and love. It is the opposite of ego. It is living in service, not living in self. It would seem so obvious then, for IHood to always seek spirit. The problem is that ego has become our ally and the familiar state of being; it is what makes us human. It has helped us survive! We are immature and we don't care. We want our needs met with immediacy.

As we mature, we begin to recognize the negative reactions of others in the self-serving ego; we recognize that if we want to have a friend, we sometimes bend to let the friend have his or her way. We eventually see that it gives us genuine pleasure, in a different way, to see someone else happy because of what we did. It is during this evolution that ego shifts to a more complicated state. It is no longer focused purely on self and skill acquisition; it sees the rival (spirit) to its self-absorption; it becomes the trickster in its fearful, life long fight against spirit. Ego is totally happy in its quest to satisfy its own neediness, and spirit is without need. The ego wants to keep IHood in selfish darkness; it wants to dominate all decisions. Light teaches us how to give love freely and experience a new level of maturity based in peace: a relief from chaos.

The mind trickster, ego, should raise a red flag in our IHood. Unfortunately, it is very clever in its approach. It is convincing and persuasive. Remember, we have had a great history of successful experiences with ego. It feels rational to satisfy the body and the ego which are powerful and physically present. Innate knowledge is usually not obvious. The spirit, because of divine free choice, does not override the ego. Thus, temptations of the flesh or need for bodily satisfaction are so powerful, the ego overtakes natural spiritual instinct based in truth. IHood knows spirit is the right minded thinker, but it is often only obvious to IHood after the ego has worked its will. At this point, we examine the situation that occurred, the consequence of our choices, and the value that we placed on the outcome. The ultimate question we can ask ourselves when we are unsure of the choice to make is, "Will I serve my interests or will I serve someone else?" If it was to serve self, it is our ego.

It is important to recognize that it is perfectly human to choose self-pleasing activities in our life. Is it self-serving to eat? Absolutely. But remember, we are physically based; taking care of our bodies is necessary to complete our divine purpose on earth. It is only when we have malicious intent that the ego monster must be thwarted. If we have love in our hearts for ourselves or for others, then we are in joyful territory, where peace will reign.

Influence of Motivation

As I've said, dependence eventually evolves to a support system based in mutual love. There are potentially many challenges to our development when, as children, there is no love. The scenarios of loveless children are not predictable but they most certainly have gloomy outcomes. The only manifestation of happiness for a loveless existence is physical and temporary. If children survive, they will spend their lives seeking love, which is a primordial motivator.

Motivation is often seen as an energy force fulfilled because of a lack. This may change as we recognize what we have. As we develop our abilities and talents, we find personal growth and fulfillment in our achievements, satisfying both ego and spirit. When we are motivated to use our gifts to the maximum, with humility and without thought of self, it is a win-win situation for the path we seek.

Reader Reflections

Reader Reflections

3
Be an Instrument of Love

Teach Life Lessons

SERVING AS AN INSTRUMENT of love requires a total commitment to practice in our daily behaviors. If we have been following the progress of maturation from earlier years, this is a natural step to take. If we have a complete understanding of love, and how to give and receive it, then we are capable of living this example, teaching others through our own expression of unconditional love.

The nature of love in our society is difficult to discuss without first addressing how we categorize it according to different levels of maturation. Conditional love rules over our relationships from childhood, perhaps even into adulthood. We love others dependent on what we get in return. Our goal however, is to express mature love, unconditional love, the ability to offer love no matter the reaction. This is a tall order, but we are able at the very least, to exhibit it as parents.

Love is difficult to define because it varies depending on the elements of the relationship. When we experience love early in life, we are immature and identify almost exclusively with the visceral feelings that accompany the emotion. It is ego controlled and thus self-serving in our initial development. As we mature, we discriminate more accurately, understanding the expectations of the other person and the needs involved. If it appears that the other loves us in a way that satisfies our needs, albeit egoic, we find satisfaction in the relationship. When this satisfaction stops, we end the relationship, especially when it is non-familial. While we are maturing, this usually serves us well. We are able to see when the other is not willing to compromise; we are certainly able to recognize when a relationship is abusive. Such a relationship is then appropriately terminated. Unfortunately, we witness some relationships that continue, reflecting a dysfunctional expression of love. These may occur because of a variety of experiences, one of which may include neglectful parents. The consequence is that children become adults who seek any kind of attention they can find, both positive and negative.

To be an instrument of love calls upon an "unconditional" loving approach toward those in our lives, especially children. We are obligated to do everything in our power to assure that we can, through our human–spirit experience, help those in our midst evolve to become the best they can be.

Life Lessons

The following is a group of lessons that I have used in workshops, classrooms, and with grandchildren. I aspire daily to find other creative ways to reach people and help them follow their intended path in life.

Talent Search

It is imperative to our existence here on earth that we uncover our individual talent and potential. Most of us can identify our strengths and weaknesses, but we need to scour the field of children's abilities. There may be latent, untapped potential. Schools also offer formal, standardized instruments to help children with this task.

When children excel in a particular area, always point it out to them. It is gratifying to the individual, and underscores their need to keep focused and develop further in that particular area of expertise. I have a word of caution however; well-meaning teachers and parents have overused praise with children, leaving them to wonder if their accolades are authentic. This practice can be confusing when we overstate another's achievement, especially if they believe the kudos to be true. They also may become over confident with their skill, becoming cocky or slacking off in their development.

Expose children to as many areas of study, sports, travel experiences, and recreational activities as possible. Infuse their worlds with music, culture and gusto for learning new things. The more exposure children have, the more likely they can find something at which they excel. I am reminded of the young baseball player who never really liked the game. His performance was lack luster, and yet he was continually encouraged to try harder. One day he discovered rowing, a less accessible sport. He loved it. He became amazingly coordinated and strong. His talents fit the sport perfectly. He is highly valued by his teammates. Crew has given him the opportunity to excel and feel confidence, which in turn has rewarded him with a generous amount of self-esteem. If not for his discovery, he might have always felt he was a poor athlete.

Providing our children with a jump start academically if they seem to be ready for it, can benefit them long term. I know of two young children who were introduced to reading at an early age. One experienced great frustration and the other excelled.

Though we can't always anticipate the outcome, it is beneficial to start young and gauge aptitude in academic areas since a child's self-esteem may be at risk. The frustrated student perhaps was not ready to read, or had a temporary disorder like dyslexia. He found that he excelled in math, however. He soon recognized that he was not incapable intellectually, and he now feels good about school.

Interestingly, some teachers believe that because of a "lack" of ability in one area, a student should focus more on the achievement of skills in the area of lack. Others believe that more time should be spent on the academic strengths of the child, but not to the exclusion of developing a set of skills in the weak study area. In any case, intellectually, we often find that we are aligned with either language skills or scientific skills. Some students are lucky to have both.

There are those who may have a great desire to become something that physically they cannot achieve. For example, a child with a large physique will likely have difficulty excelling in ballet. A small-framed child may not be successful in football. This is not to say these children should be dissuaded from spreading their metaphorical wings, but it is more realistic and helpful to explain to them why they may not be as successful with the results of their efforts. Physical attributes have a bearing on success in sports often because the very nature of the sport dictates certain body types are more inclined to succeed.

Doing a Takeover

There is a new practice that is rewarding in helping teach behavioral outcomes. The "take over" is a technique whereby one gets a second chance at expressing themselves, when the first time was hurtful. It demonstrates how to communicate more positively with others. If a child is reactive or rude, he or she may find the outcome of their behavior is a negative, equally reactive one. For example, brother confronts sister when she retrieves the last cookie. He calls her fat, but her reaction is equally inflammatory, and the conversation snowballs into a storm of callous words and hurtful criticisms. With a parent nearby to mediate, they are afforded another try with a "take over". This time, brother asks sister if she would be willing to share the cookie. If she says yes, it is a win. If she says no, he loses the cookie option under provisions of the house rules, which state: "whoever gets it first can have it." However, the longer term solution would bet on the sister cooperating knowing that, next time, she may not reach the last cookie first.

A Box of Rocks

A social worker friend of mine who works as a therapist was telling me about a beautiful exercise she employs to bring groups together, and to help individuals realize their greatest gift in life is love. She finds an exquisite box and puts several dozen polished rocks or gems inside. At the end of the exercise, each participant chooses a rock to take home to remember the experience.

I expanded on this idea to include a "bonding" experience among our grandchildren on a "grandparents" weekend. Only those kids eight years old and older were included, because of their maturity level. We went to a highly energized, huge rock (sometimes referred to as a vortex) situated several feet above the St. Lawrence River in upstate New York. It is a magical place.

We gathered, cross legged, on the ground while I explained that I had something very special in my box. I asked them to pass the unopened box around the circle. When they held the box, they concentrated and sent as much love as they could muster into it. It was a special moment for all of us, and I was struck at the intensity and time each beautiful soul used, trusting that it was going to be very special. When the box came back to me, I placed it in the center of our circle and opened it. They seemed surprised to see a mere mound of rocks. I acknowledged their reaction, but invited them to choose any one of these rocks to keep forever. It would remind them of the special gift of love from each of their cousins, and they would always remember this time together.

It took a very long time for each of them to choose their rock. They took great pleasure pouring through their choices. Some took small pebble sized stones, and others took the biggest they could find. They touched them, held them, and sized them up until they found their "special one." This was a heartfelt moment for me as well. There was a warm, loving smile on each of their faces, a reflection of a special day and loving memory.

Bluebirds of Happiness

The same therapist also shared an idea she used for clients who were having difficulties in life. She found small replicas of bluebirds and bought them for her clients. The idea was to give people positive alternatives to negative thinking. They can look at the small bluebird and choose to have a good day over a bad one. This same little token is also given to clients who seem to be progressing. It is her way of saying that she sees more happiness in them.

This exercise may not seem life shattering, but it is one more technique to communicate in a positive way. I suggest parents buy something similar for their children; or perhaps let them pick it out. It empowers them to choose the symbol of positive communication between the two of you.

What does this say to our children? "You are the most important person in my world and you come first at this moment. I promise not to judge you. I will listen without criticism. When you are done, I will respond to you. I may not be happy, but I won't be reactive. If you have a problem, I will help you in any way I can, even if it's just to listen."

Trust me; this approach will work, especially with teens! The earlier in life you start the process, the more effective the outcome.

Wearing Our Masks

As mentioned earlier, humans use masks to please egos; we are either trying to impress someone or get something we want. It isn't a healthy habit, but it's been effective in our lifetimes. Usually, when we mature enough to understand the folly of this behavior and trust our authentic selves, we live in the truth of who we are. It is the best choice for all that we do.

To help children, or even adults, to see the benefit of unmasking, here is an exercise that I have devised that at least brings light to the choices we can make.

At Halloween time a few years ago, I purchased a bunch of masks to be used by participants in this exercise. I passed out the masks and explained how we falsely present ourselves in given situations. We hide behind this false face to cover up what we see to be a less positive image of who we are. We sit quietly and let this concept seep into a pretend world. I had a mask on, too, and I began talking about how much easier it was at that moment to communicate with everyone because I had this protection on my face; I didn't feel exposed. It made the group less frightening and intimidating to me. I could be something other than who I was in that moment. For example, it allowed me to invent myself for the crowd.

Each person had a chance to speak to the group about how they felt under the mask. Then we took them off and formed pairs. I asked to have a private conversation about whether they thought they might be doing this in their lives. Doing this one on one is less threatening because it is difficult to reveal personal weakness to a larger group.

There is no judgment involved in this activity. It is simply a technique to help people be aware of what we may be doing that is keeping us from a more peaceful, honest behavioral pattern. This may be an effective and educational practice for a family. It is important that siblings don't point accusatory fingers at other siblings or at a parent. This is not intended to be incriminating. It is a loving, gentle way of saying to the people we love, "Look at this. Do we do this? Is it holding us back from true happiness?"

Ceremony of Love

In *Sharing the Medicine of Love*[2] a book I co-authored with Val Cook, we talk about a special way to honor those we love in our lives, including family, friends, and even strangers. We may not love them in the same way, but our love is expansive as we mature. Val created this ceremony for her granddaughters to celebrate their menses. However, it can be used for any number of reasons: birthdays, anniversaries, even tragedy. In fact, I have said to people with loved ones who are ill, "use it as a eulogy for those who need to hear the extent to which we love them." Better we all experience that before we die. It gives everyone an opportunity to share innermost feelings; it is a beautiful experience.

Those who are honoring gather in a semi-circle around the guest of honor; and begin the celebration by touching his or her face and forehead with a warm, damp cloth, or aromatic oils. With

---

2   Cook and Little, *Sharing the Medicine of Love*, 2008

each touch, we express our love, honoring them for how they have touched our lives and hearts.

At the end of the celebration the honoree is wrapped with a shawl as the attendees demonstrate their love and respect. The celebrant then keeps the shawl to use whenever they feel a need for love in their life. It is a source of comfort, and a reminder to them of how many people they have touched and how much they are loved.

This exercise is life changing and forever memorable to those who have participated. A more thorough description of the ceremony and its uses can be found in *Sharing the Medicine of Love*.

Reader Reflections

Reader Reflections

4
Living Our IHood

Judgment, Choosing Our Battles, and the Masks We Wear

IHOOD, AS WE MATURE, becomes very adept at making judgments of self and others.

Unfortunately, there is a point at which we begin to use judgment to measure ourselves against others, especially when we begin to believe how "special" we are, compared to them. We begin by measuring our prowess, which is usually physical ("I can throw a ball farther than anyone in my class" or "I am the worst athlete in my class"). We may compare our strengths and weaknesses, which is ultimately destructive. The problem arises when our internal examination ends with the conclusion that we can never be perfect enough.

This thought process extends to others when we view them as not meeting our expectations; for example, parents. We see their flaws and pick at their weaknesses because they are not the person we have created them to be. Then, as adults, we begin to correct others "for their own good." Our ego demands it. Our free will chooses to judge, and ego urges us to point out the weaknesses we see in them (especially as compared to our own).

Usually we see our children as a complete reflection of us.

This is endearing until we realize that they are not as "perfect" as we are, so we set out to correct their flaws too. One can easily see the folly in this thinking. Until we fully mature in our life, it is difficult to accept that we cannot and should not set out to change others into our personal definition of "perfection."

If we have a mature perspective, we recognize when we are serving our self and not respecting others, thereby living outside of our integrity. It takes great perseverance to compassionately accept the human nature that is in all of us. As we aspire to our IHood, we align with our spirit-wisdom ("My daughter feels so badly she spilled milk on your table. It was an accident. I will clean it up") and less to egoic thought ("Oh no. My daughter spilled milk all over your table. I'm so embarrassed!"). We come to realize we humans cannot improve upon God's perfection. It is wise to remember the words of Jesus, "Judge not lest ye be judged" (Matt 7:1, KJV).

> For with the judgment you pronounce you will be judged, and the measure you give will be the measure you get. Why do you see the speck in your brother's eye, but do not notice the log in your own eye? Or, how can you say to your brother, "Let me take the speck out of your eye," when there is the log in your own eye? You hypocrite, first take the log out of your own eye, and then you will see clearly to take the speck out of your brother's eye.
>
> (Matt 7:2–5, RSV)

The remarkable phenomenon about being judgmental is that we are critical of others for the same issues that we dislike in ourselves, sometimes unconsciously. In our drive for perfection, we elevate our status by pointing out another's imperfection. Those who "rub us the wrong way" are actually our teachers. The next time you are ready to criticize, observe the issue and think about what is sparking your discomfort. Then (and this is not an easy exercise) mentally embrace the other person for being a teacher. Correct in yourself what you are challenged by in them. Notice the ego involvement that has surfaced. I find this one of the most uncomfortable practices in my pursuit of consciousness in spirit.

Choosing Our Battles

In the pursuit of spiritual domination for our IHood, it is important to do some self-examination with regard to our effort to control others and the world in general. Because we falsely believed that we were in control in our younger years, we strive to gain or regain more of that control as we get older. The taste of power over others is addictive. Problems arise when we try to reign over others by inappropriately making decisions for them that are rightfully theirs to make. We rationalize our egoic behavior toward others by convincing ourselves that they don't have the experience we have to make such decisions. Those consumed with this activity have perhaps heard themselves referred to as "control freaks." If this sounds familiar, remember, this behavior pattern of ego is not really for the good of the other; it is for the destruction of what *we* don't want in the other so that we can continue to view them as incompetent or inexperienced, not as capable.

Control freak behavior is not always obvious to us. To check, ask yourselves: how many times have I exclaimed, "Watch out for that car!" or, "You're going too fast!"? How many parents have badgered their child for the smallest infraction? For example, "Get your elbows off the table and sit up straight. When will it stick in that thick skull of yours?" There will be a point when the child turns them off. Sometimes it's okay to just look the other way. Yes, manners are important, but have faith that your child will eventually surprise you when you least expect it! My mother use to say, "Don't worry, your son won't slurp his soup by the time he's in college." She was right.

A successful practice for those of us hell bent on correcting and controlling people around us is to pick the battles that we have in our lives; otherwise, we will live lives filled with catfights and emotional bruises. When we don't get our way or are met with resistance, we may be wise to stand aside. IHood recognizes, eventually, that the ego doesn't have all the answers but it does have the energy to create them. It is pointless to spend time brooding over others' imperfections and to practice defending our reasons for our next "I'm in charge" moment. It is a time waster and a gut wrenching practice for all parties involved. It only produces chaos for us and for those around us.

We need to let go of ego and listen to truth spirit, respecting and allowing others' rights to be in control, and to allow others to make mistakes. We all need to discover our own frailties, knowing that by stumbling, we strengthen our legs for the next climb. Our IHood can evoke the art of becoming an observer as we evolve. By staying quiet and watchful, acknowledging spirit's truth, we gain wisdom.

Masks We Wear

Masks are ego protectors and ego builders. We wear them from the time we recognize that we're rewarded or punished for behaving in a certain way or in a certain circumstance. We begin to use our masks to gain praise and, in some cases, punishment. The sole purpose of the mask is for the ego to gain the attention that it is seeking at that moment. The mask we wear is the person we become for the "other" person, be it a parent, a friend, or a teacher; whoever in our life requires us to wear a false face. This mask is worn for the sole purpose of gaining approval or improving our egoic image and winning through feeling superior and privileged. If the mask we create doesn't receive the expected or desired outcome we are seeking, then we change the mask appropriately for the next encounter or experience. It is always the intent of the ego mask to elevate and enrich self.

Some simple examples of wearing a mask might be a child trying to please Mommy, wearing his "best behavior mask" because he wants the squirt gun for his birthday. Then there is the child who doesn't get the candy at the checkout counter. He becomes enraged, with the hope that a parent will give in to the "tantrum mask," especially if it has worked in the past when Mother gave into her embarrassment.

Masks are created with frequency in younger years, and they survive as a mechanism of egoic success into adolescence and adulthood. This behavior has much to do with self-confidence and we have habituated this technique to the point of losing our authentic selves.

As others' behaviors toward us change, then our ego may feel the need to reinvent the face we present until the desired outcome is found. This can result in tragedy if we change our truth, or authenticity. For example, how many of us marry or gain a partner that we want by becoming what we think the future partner is looking for, rather than being the genuine person that we are in truth? It soon becomes difficult if not impossible to keep up the charade of this mask we have invented to be appealing and loveable to the partner. We can recognize the destruction in this scenario, for both parties will ultimately suffer, even though the ego got what it wanted. The true spirit is denied.

Each stage of development finds a new and changing mask to represent our new persona. We have seen adolescents behaving very mannerly and grown up at the dinner table and the next moment slamming doors because they couldn't have the family car. It is inconsistent and persists until they recognize that it is not necessary or appropriate to continue in this manner. It is destructive, rather than healing, chaotic rather than peaceful. When IHood becomes dominated by spirit, we stop feeding the faces of ego. The goal is to eventually remove our masks and reveal our genuine self, consistently and confidently. Our authentic self is our natural state, the spiritual vestige that entered our human body at our birth. We are free of egoic corruption.

Reaching adulthood does not automatically result in a demonstration of mature behavior. It is possible, and sometimes probable, that ego is still completely dominant. Many of us enter into marriage or parenthood too early, without the maturity or development of spiritual enlightenment necessary for a mature loving relationship. When we are involved in a relationship outside of self, it is imperative to have the ability to put others first. This is how we know if we are ready for marriage and children. If the ego is in total control, it is not possible to compromise or give love unconditionally. Only IHood awareness of spirit and the Light can supply selfless love. We can all attest to the broken lives that are created through immature relationships. The tragedy is underscored when children are involved.

We are operating predominantly in spirit when we are brave enough to take the mask off permanently. There is no need to ask ourselves why we find it necessary to wear them in the first place. It is an alias that we give ourselves while trying on our dreams. Eventually we realize it's just a cover up for our real self. We should look forward to our unveiling, since we are the unique creation of God.

Reader Reflections

5
Our Divine Human Spirit
The Free Will Challenge

WE MAY NEVER KNOW when our life's work is at hand; when pure spirit takes over and we are complete in our mission. There was a young man who probably didn't know what his life's purpose was to be. He was a Navy SEAL who saved the lives of his comrades by throwing himself on top of a grenade thrown at them by Iraqi insurgents. If you ask the men whose lives he saved, this was his defining moment. Many would argue that his was a senseless death. He was a twenty five year old hero. What a miracle if we could find our purpose, perform our responsibility on this earth, and stop senseless suffering in the process. Thank you, Petty Officer Second Class Michael A. Monsoor. We will never know what he was thinking when he performed such unparalleled heroism, but we do know our Creator asks something of each of us when we enter this world and it was not in vain that he died, serving his country, his fellow man, and the Light.

Humans have the same spirit given to Moses, Abraham, and Jesus. These holy men were full of spirit, but living a human existence as well. We are living with the same divine compass.

Our recognition, acknowledgment, and acceptance of our divine purpose may come through at any time and at any speed; it can be gradual or take a split second, as it was for Michael Monsoor.

Our Creator stamps our purpose into our DNA. But when we are born, there are obstacles that we must overcome in order to reach our path to purpose. We have to grow up physically and emotionally to grow "into" a spirituality that eagerly waits to be sought out. We have to overcome the temptations of being an ego filled human.

> For the whole law is fulfilled in one word, "You shall love your neighbor as yourself" ... but if you bite and devour one another take heed that you are not consumed by one another ... walk by the Spirit, and so not gratify the flesh ... for the desires of the flesh are against the Spirit, and the desires of the Spirit are against the flesh; for these are opposed to each other to prevent you from doing what you would.
>
> (Paul to the Galatians, 5:14)

It is our divine destiny to sort and pick our way through life to find our purpose, and to help humankind.

During our maturation, we undergo challenges while we acquire life skills and God given talent. We have to learn how to live in our society, to gain the perspective and maturity to withstand what is asked of us. We have to learn to traverse life's bumpy road and its inevitable hurdles.

In the early part of the twentieth century, Psychologist Erik Erikson, studied the development of the human race for clues to how we advance in our own humanity. He studied with Anna

Freud, Sigmund Freud's daughter, and taught at many prestigious universities, including Harvard Medical School, Berkeley, and Yale. His research on human development included childhood, adolescence, adulthood, and old age. His findings were reported in his "Eight Ages of Man"[3], more commonly referred to as Erikson's Eight Developmental Stages.

Erikson's belief was that each stage of development points to a crisis that has to be resolved in order to evolve to the next stage of development. He coined the term "identity crisis," commonly used today to describe the time of intense self-examination when we discover different ways of looking at ourselves.

Early on in these stages, Erikson believed that we develop the ego identity, which is described as the "conscious" sense of self. He believed that this ego identity changed constantly as we gained new information about our social interactions, and our experiences, and ourselves.

Erikson also believed that as competency improved throughout life's stages, individuals gain a mastery that affects the ego's strength and quality. Conversely, if this improvement did not occur, a lack of competency would lead to inadequacies in a variety of areas.

Erikson felt the need for expansion of his theory later in life to include more than the worldly view. He felt there was more to uncover.

He once said, "Hope is both the earliest and the most indispensable virtue inherent in the state of being alive. If life is to be sustained, hope must remain, even where confidence is wounded, trust impaired"[4].

In other words, there is a way to survive our developmental

---

3   International Journal of Psychiatry, Vol 2 (3), 1966, 281-300
4   The Erik Erikson Reader, 2000

flaws, despite the scars and the bruising we carry through life. Something else drives us.

It is my belief that the hope, or "thing," that keeps us alive on earth, is our spirit. It is the spirit, not the ego, which keeps us conscious in our lives … We are usually not aware of our spirit until after our ego does its job, which initially is necessary for our earthly development. Because the ego presents itself early in our formative years, it gets a hold on our identity. It is only later, as we mature, that we recognize that our ego is the potential cause of our chaos and self-destruction. Ego keeps us in an "unconscious" state as we react to our world.

IHood finds that, with maturity, we no longer have to be reactive. Reactivity is aligned with ego. When we discover our divine spirituality, there is no reason to react, since our perspective is not ego minded. Spirituality leads us to peace; the mindset needed to self-actualize and live in our natural state: the place of our purpose in this world. IHood helps us understand how we evolve to spirit and successfully acclimate to our human existence.

The ego and spirituality are constantly trying to reach the proper balance while residing in our IHood, within our human body. Saint Paul writes of this phenomenon:

> What is sown a natural body, rises a spiritual body. If there is a natural body, there is a spiritual body. So also it is written, the first man, Adam, became a living soul; the last Adam became a life giving spirit. But it is not the spiritual that comes first, but the physical, and then the spiritual … Therefore, even as we have borne the likeness of the earthy, let us bear also the likeness of the heavenly.
>
> (Corinthians, 15:44)

Erikson spoke of an identity crisis: the state in which we find ourselves when we don't know who we are in this world. This is because we are not mature enough to awaken to our spiritual presence. We are ego driven and seeking bodily satisfaction, to which the body was born. Once we are sufficiently cognizant of love that is other than selfish love, we become open to our divine spirit.

In our culture, *love* is only one word, with many definitions. In Greek, the following are the words for love:

Storge (pronounced stor-geh): love between parents and children
Philia: love between friends
Eros: love of somebody to get something from them; selfish love
Agape (pronounced a-gah peh): unselfish love; loving others

It would be great if we had similar separate meanings in English for these various manifestations of love, but it suffices to say that we understand there are different meanings we assign to this magnificent word. The mature love that we express for others, without expectation of a return benefit for self, often referred to as *unconditional love*, is that which opens the door to our spiritual existence and the Light that guides us to our purpose.

IHood is the fulcrum on which we intellectually balance between ego domination of our mind and the divine living spirit that was placed in our soul. It allows us to hear the messages of ego and the messages of spirit. It then allows us to invoke the power of free will in our earthly action. IHood allows us to manifest our destiny; to fully realize our perfect dream by overcoming human obstacles through love and light.

We are divine by creation but we are placed in a human world. IHood is the unique guidance system used to find our ultimate reason for living. It is the interpreter of present moments, the translator of past experiences, and the acknowledger of expectations for the future. It keeps us in touch with the Light in its consciousness. Otherwise, we would forever be in identity crisis, always identifying with self-serving accomplishments. We would live with short term, feel good solutions rather than those that may take a lifetime to reach and benefit humankind.

Our lives do not require fame or fortune. Our reward is love, peace, and joy. All we have to do is listen closely to our "inner voice" and begin to transform using our IHood.

We all have this inner voice. As Mahatma Gandhi once said, "Everyone who wills can hear the inner voice. It is within everyone[5]."

We hear spirit when it speaks to us, just as we hear the ego. The difference is that the spirit says, "Open the door for that poor woman who is struggling with her cane." The ego says, "Cut that car off; it just honked at you and you didn't deserve that treatment!"

When we are created, we are in total consciousness, filled with the potential of endless love, which is spiritually based. Once our Creator places our potential in our physical bodies, we undergo the plight of survival of our spirituality inside our human flesh condition. We must accommodate and acclimate to our parents and our physical surrounding; begin to synthesize our skill and ability levels, and recognize our potential as we progress. We must sort and choose as we initially survive. We must discover how our IHood works, changing our motivational field as we transform from an ego dominated life (needed in the beginning years of our life) to that of spiritual domination. In IHood, we change from our

---

5   BrainyQuote.com, 2012

need driven survival to that of divine choosing, exercising free will as God has intended, choosing to live our purpose, accomplished by loving unconditionally.

The journey of growing up and fully reaching maturity presents difficulties that become apparent during our social, physical, and psychological changes. As we become aware of "me," the struggle silently begins between our ego identity, and our spirituality. The body and its needs are dominant at this point in our development and it is apparent that the spiritual domination at birth is no longer recognized. The spirit never leaves our soul, or IHood, for that matter; it just goes into a waiting period where it is dormant, waiting for its awakening; being patient for maturity to reunite us with the conscious state we had before our birth. The extent to which our maturation is successfully completed determines how quickly we regain our full knowledge of purpose, which dismisses the unconscious behavior of an ego controlled mind. The eight stages of maturation are important in understanding the development of IHood and how as humans, we begin to recognize that there is more in our world than just our own selves. This is when initial recognition of spiritual existence begins.

Since our spirituality is always with us, we might wonder why we face such a developmental challenge. It is because of free will. It is divined to us, just like our spirit. We are given the ability to make decisions between choices in our lives. Some choices are inconsequential while others are of far greater import. The younger we are, the less mature we are, and thus are less aware of the consequences of our decisions. This is why parental guidance is so necessary. During our formative years, parents are thus essential in their role of helping us as we grow. Parents are the mature caretakers of the earth's children.

Though it would seem that parents' presence and influence are most important when children are younger, it is not necessarily so. Challenges are present in all stages of maturity, and in fact may be more critical at later stages of adolescence, before reaching adulthood. It's critical to mention, too, that the single most important component of the parenting role is the nurturing and love that must surround a child. It is the blessed oil that lubricates the successful journey through maturation and ultimately provides the success in finding one's purpose in this life.

If the body is deprived, or if IHood perceives that it is deprived, the ego becomes dominant, since it identifies with all that is physical and self-serving. The spirit, though present, is dependent on the ascent to a minimal level of maturity so that it is heard within IHood and communicates its presence to ego.

In the following chapters, you are invited on a new journey to explore the powerful development of the ego, discussed first using Erikson's research, and later, the impact of motivation as derived from Maslow's *Hierarchy of Need*.[6] There will be more discussion on how IHood plays its part in the eternal battle between self-serving behavior and spirit-serving behavior, using the power of free will. The mature outcome transforms the dominance of ego to spirit, righting the wrong minded thinking that our ego uses to create chaos in our lives. It is then that IHood chooses spirit more and more. This is when the spiritual mind is in charge, and we are able to fully live our purpose. It is my belief that those capable of achieving total transformation to spiritually based, free will choices are the likes of Gandhi, Pope John Paul II, and Mother Teresa. They are the saints who are models for living our purpose.

---

6   1943, *A Theory of Human Motivation*

6
Who Am I?

A Self-Assessment

WE NEED TO KNOW who we are: our biological needs; our perception of ourselves, our family and social arena; the level of our abilities to survive and create; our potential to give and receive love; our intellectual capacity; our spiritual connectedness; these are some of the self-revealing attributes that are necessary to find our path in life.

Unfortunately, once we "inventory" who we are, we can't file it away and go on with life. Self-discovery is constant and changing. We carry the joys and the burdens of our struggles from the time of our birth. We constantly test our authenticity. It isn't as simple as taking a look in the mirror to see who we are; IHood is far more complex.

When we assess who we are, it can be painful; there are times in our maturing years that were more difficult than we want to remember. We may find that we are not quite "finished" in our quest for maturity. This doesn't mean we are hopelessly doomed. We are all perfectly capable of seeking more understanding and changing our personal behavior. God has created in us the challenge of becoming the best we can be. In our maturity, we can fulfill this mission.

If we find our problems seem insurmountable, it is wise to seek professional help. It is ill advised to tackle severe personal conflict. This exercise is not meant to be used for self-torment or to assign blame for a self-perceived failure, nor is it an opportunity to victimize ourselves. Rather, self-assessment is an aid to understanding where we stumbled in our maturation process. This has the potential to open up possibilities for personal growth. The human brain is designed with capacity to store memories; memories that record past decisions and are revisited when we are confronted to make new ones. The memory function enables us to make better decisions based on those that may not have served us well in the past. It provides us the opportunity to break out of previous prohibitive behavioral patterns, thereby steering us closer toward our purpose. Over time, as these memories are revisited and we make different decisions under similar circumstances, we can re-wire our brains and that reaction becomes more automatic. Our IHood has been tapped.

The following questions will help you review your journey up to now. It will help to gain perspective of your life and understand your motivation. There is no right or wrong answer; there is no judgment of what should or should not have been accomplished. Assess where you are in life right now. Perhaps you are exactly where you want to be; life may be full of contentment and peace. However, if you have excessive chaos and lack happiness, then you may think about where to change your behavior or situation. Use a journal to review the answers afterwards. For further introspection, it is suggested that you ask "Why?" after each of the following questions.

1. Do I routinely feel a sense of trust and hope in my life, or am I more fearful and suspicious?

2. Am I capable of developing friendships easily?
3. Do I sufficiently exercise self-control?
4. Am I confident in my intellectual, physical, and social skills?
5. Do I feel a need to be the center of attention?
6. Do I feel competent or inferior with my accomplishments?
7. Am I able to be independent (alone), or must I always have someone in my life?
8. Do I avoid commitment or do I express love to others freely?
9. Am I concerned for my family (society) more than for myself, or am I self-indulgent?
10. Am I fulfilled in life, or am I in despair?

The answers we provide will help us to understand how well we have matured and developed through our life stages. It will be beneficial to read chapters 8 through 12 to understand how maturity affects our behavior at different stages in life. If we are able to reach full maturity through our life cycle, we are able to express our spiritual capability as well, leading us to complete our life's work.

There is a great emphasis on social adjustment, which is extremely important because we are not alone on earth. We need to learn how to cooperate and work democratically toward goals that better humankind. The interaction we have is often key to our own recognition of whether we are self-centered (egoic) or "other" centered (spiritual), as previously discussed. The degree to which we make an adequate social adjustment in our family, neighborhood, community, and the world, has a large bearing on who we become and the friends we choose. Our friends may be, in fact, reflections of what we believe our own identity to be.

Friendships that we make are also related to how we spend our time.

The following questions are suggested for your contemplation:

1. Who are my friends?
2. Do I like them?
3. Why do I like being with them?
4. Am I similar to them?

Now consider these questions:
1. What do I like to do?
2. Where and how do I spend my time?
3. What are my aspirations?
4. Am I moving toward my goals, or standing still?

We may realize that what we think we like, we don't like at all; what we do with our time is not what we really want to do. We may not be internally aligned with our external behavior. We may also find we possess some unattractive traits, and we may not be willing to change them. Recognize that they are a part of us, but we challenge ourselves to reach our evolvement.

If we are fair to ourselves, we can accept our perfections and imperfections and still know that we are loveable creations. God loved us enough to give us our life and these gifts. If we see them with dissatisfaction, then this is an opportunity to strive to improve where we can, and work with acceptance of what we can't change. We can accept the challenge of developing our potential, and to flower from the seed of our creation into the life force that we are intended to be.

An honest evaluation of our abilities is necessary in this self-assessment; it is the only way we can discern between reality and fantasy. We need to ask "am I using all the tools I have been given?" If we are in pursuit of who we really are, we will have better focus. We can dismiss the things that are unimportant and circumstantial in our lives; dismiss that which we do not have the gifts to attain. Then we can proceed to accept our life's potential and update our "discoveries" of strengths and weaknesses in all areas. This allows us to develop fully. It will also keep us in reality. (If we are seven feet tall and weigh three hundred pounds, we know it to be unrealistic to train as a ballet dancer.)

Sometimes we are convinced that we do not have talent in a certain area, like art or music, when we really do. When I was in high school, I had an art teacher who told me I had absolutely no talent. I had to agree with her when she pointed out that my houses on the hill would have rolled down the hill had they been built the way I drew them. They sure didn't look like real houses. Seven years ago, however, I took a class at the Scottsdale Artists School in Arizona, at my husband's urging. We enrolled in sculpture, taught by John Coleman, an extremely successful and accomplished Cowboy Artist. Though my husband was an artist, he had never taken sculpture either. To my great surprise, I was quite talented! In fact, I made several bronzes and went on to do several oil portraits of my grandchildren as well. The lesson for me was to recognize that, with maturity and motivation, we might find abilities where we thought there were none. Never give up the opportunity to try something new, even if you failed in the past.

The rewards we feel from accomplishment and outside approval are desirable for us at any point in life. Think of the child who is looking for applause for the first steps taken; or the child who recites a poem at her first assembly, with cheers that follow. These are egoic pursuits that are neither destructive nor malicious. In fact, ego plays an important role in our skill development, especially in the early years.

As we grow up, we undergo different stages in our lives that present particular challenges we must endure (acquire an education, learn behavioral expectations, and develop God given skills). This is the responsibility and promise of our human experience: the direction we must go in order to grow in life and awaken to our potential. It is then that we can become instruments of love. Our challenge is to discover the gifts unique to us and give them to those who need them.

When we are even slightly aware of the reason for our journey, we maintain a stronger spiritual connection. It doesn't mean that we abandon our worldly responsibilities; it simply allows us to ascend to a higher level of contribution in our world. Carlos Slim, a man from Mexico, on the Forbes list of richest people in the world, exemplifies how we can live an extraordinary life. It was with interest that I watched his interview with Larry King on the Fox Network in December of 2010.

Mr. Slim applies his accumulated wealth in ways that benefit others: educational scholarships and an art museum for the public. He also lives in a modest home because he says that in a very large home he would not see his children easily or often. He also enjoys his outdoor gardens where he believes true beauty is found.

He says that when we start out in life, we want to acquire stuff. If we are lucky, we get more and more and more. Then we realize that our happiness has not increased threefold; all we need is time with our family, which is the center of our happiness. Mr. Slim also said we need to pass on the understanding that more is not better; it starts by teaching children. It is important not to buy them more and more toys. They will not play with what they have, and they will only want more. The concept of "we need more" is a big mistake we make in our lives.

We can learn much from this man's example. Ask yourself

how you are living your life. Is it with the goal of gaining the stuff of this world or for the benefit of bringing joy and comfort to others?

It is important to find our conviction: our truth, what we believe in. Discover what gifts we possess, and use them; not only in our vocation, but also in our avocation, in our entire life. Are we artists who portray compassion that speaks to others' souls? Do we have the aptitude to teach and guide children? Do we have business acumen that awards us the financial resources to use for charity? How are we able to transform to our calling? What characteristics do we possess that make us an instrument of God's love?

When we can evolve to our highest calling, we will answer, "Yes, that's who I am."

Reader Reflections

7
Human Development with Spiritual Implications
IHood and Maturation

IT IS ESSENTIAL THAT we attain maturity in our formative years in order to moderate our ego, embrace our spirit, and fully evolve to a productive, peaceful life.

Maturation is critical to IHood, and Erik Erikson is instrumental in explaining why it is.

Erik Erikson was a social scientist who took a dramatic step toward researching how we develop as human beings, resulting in his groundbreaking theories as articulated in *Eight Stages of Man.* Dr. Erikson dealt with the social and psychological aspects of our maturity, seeking to discover the mystery of self-identity and personality development. Erikson studied with Anna Freud and expanded his theories beyond Sigmund Freud's psychosexual stages of development. Erikson's theory has been instrumental in the understanding of children and learning theory, and is invaluable to educators, parents, and those interested in how we grow up within society.

Erikson's research has always been a guidepost for me as I taught young children in my earlier career, and I advanced his theory to the future teachers I taught at the college level from the 1970s until the mid-1990s. It has become obvious to me that there is a critical dimension of how humans interact and grow up that is missing in Erikson's explanations: it is the spiritual dimension of our existence. Hope, virtue, values, and ethics are not discussed in any weighty manner, other than to explain that a child's moral maturity seems to be explained by the adult pressures in a child's life, which Erikson refers to as the "guilt culture." Erikson, of course, was not the only person who held the belief that morality is an imposed behavioral agreement we have devised to keep order in our society. Many behavioral scientists have clung to this explanation, perhaps out of necessity, since a spiritual explanation typically has been wrought with complications for the scientific community. However, much evidence indicates that this is changing and, in fact, science is starting to catch up to understanding the incredible dynamic of spirituality.

The spiritual dimension, in my view, absolutely needs to be discussed with regard to maturation, since it significantly impacts behavioral development and the outcome of our life. It accounts for our morality and our search for living a higher purpose as we mature. When this spiritual dimension is included, it helps us to close the gaps in our quest for understanding certain behavior and to answer the question of "Why are we here?" that is addressed through maturity.

There is more than the spiritual veneer to this discussion. Logically, it would seem that if we did not have the divine in our soul, we would never ask the question of why we are here; in fact, we might not even care. We would not see the love emanating from the elderly man when a puppy licks his hand in the nursing home or feel the solitude and comfort of the wind blowing through the pines. If we were merely of this world and just in an ego dominated body and mind, we would purely be in a self-serving world, living daily to meet the next need, whatever it may be. Some would argue that is, in fact, how we are. We are doing battle in a dog eat dog world, running red lights to beat the other guy to the next one. But we know there is more than the "next immediate fix," and that spirit rescues us from our egoism. It is always with us. We are hard wired with spirit before we ever enter our body.

Coming into a physical world with a divine spirit is a challenge to us all; our body is of the earth; our spirit is of the divine Creator. So we are constantly being tugged by two different "masters." We look at a beautiful new baby, with perfect fingers and toes, consider the miracle of creation, and feel the complete joy that new life brings. Yet, two hours later, we lament that this little interloper is crying, exhausting us and interrupting our quiet.

The acknowledged presence of spirit offers a different impact and new view upon maturation theory and upon how we grow up. It actually helps us understand why there is such complexity! As we get further into the discussion of how we grow up, we will see that immaturity is closely aligned with ego and our maturity is identified with the divine. By examining the characteristics of ego and spirit within our behavior, we have a clearer understanding of IHood.

The notion of the divine spirit within us is not my idea, as we all know. It is a concept that is accepted in the belief systems of most major religions in our world: Hinduism, Judaism, Christianity, and Islam. This divine spirit is a permanent player in our moral development. It is the spine of our integrity and the leader of virtue. It is awakened by the love that the Creator has gifted us and which binds us together in our divine humanity. While Erikson believed that the child has a moral maturity inflicted by adult pressures in his or her life, I believe our soul takes over as it is awakened during our maturity and becomes our "mature" compass in life; in modern terms, our GPS. We are quite capable, in fact, of taking the reins of our own moral development. Initially, as children, we may resist the moral inspiration of our souls because of our immaturity and ego centeredness, but we have the potential to reach maturity fully and thus awaken to our purpose through divine spirit, as we gain responsibility for ourselves.

Furthermore, to note, spirit is not a stage of maturation. The spirit is present at our conception and departs, intact in our soul, at the end of our mortal life. It is always present, but not always "seen," recognized, or acknowledged in our humanity. Our soul communicates with us through the mind and awakens in our soul through love; our ego also communicates to us through our mind, but resides in our body.

As I said earlier, it is interesting that social scientists have never included the spiritual dimension in any discussions regarding human development. I believe that its omission is due to at least three factors: first, educators are forbidden to include the concept of divine spirit in our teachings, even though the vast majority of our religions believe spirit to exist. This is especially true in the United States, where church and state are separated as dictated in the Constitution because of our unfortunate history with England in the 1600s. Secondly, Francis Bacon's method of scientific research, which is central to modern science, expects scientists to steer clear of trying to prove things that are not measurable. Scientists experiment and form hypotheses, using causation between phenomena based on induction. Because spirit is not clearly observable, it is difficult to find clear results. Now, newer techniques such as magnetic field studies are leading scientists more closely to acknowledging that which they could not measure in the past. Finally, social scientists who propose the existence of a higher being, let alone include such an idea within a social science theory, are at risk of being exposed to ridicule by nonbelievers, which often leads to an apologetic ministry of defending one's faith. Thus, I am exposing myself to such ridicule (gladly) since my belief in IHood is clearly faith driven.

To avoid the mention of God in our discussion because it is seen as a non-intellectual, non-scientific, non-provable view is simply going along with the crowds of even spiritual writers, who may have the same views but fear reprisals or intellectual shunning. They find safety in citing eastern philosophers, using safer synonyms or substitutes like *Light* and *Creator* exclusively, because it is not politically correct to use *God*. Rationally, however, if our belief systems acknowledge His spiritual presence in all human beings, it is folly to exclude the discussion of God and the Holy Spirit's existence.

The development of IHood embraces our spiritual dimension and better explains behaviors that were difficult to explain in the past. This spiritual dimension may very well have been what Freud was referring to in his use of "superego," which is the internalization of all the restrictions to which the ego must bow. Could it be that his superego is the existence of our divine spirit? The explanations of the intricacies of interplay between ego and spirit may be more easily understood with this correlation, though of course we all have free will to choose between egoic and spiritual behavior.

If we were only intended to live our life as a living organism, to be absorbed into the earth at death, then Freud's explanation would give us sufficient evidence of how our mind (psyche) works. C. G. Jung dared to imply that there was a more religious function to this concept, and was ignored by most in the scientific community. IHood is a plausible concept for those who embrace our purpose, which is to love and serve each other on this earth.

Reader Reflections

Reader Reflections

8
The Spiritual Neophyte
First and Second Years of Life

First Year of Life: Mother, Trust, and Potential Fear

THE FIRST SIGNIFICANT RELATIONSHIP that affects us is the one with our mother (or maternal substitute). This is the cornerstone of our development, and thus explains why it is so important that mothers, themselves, be sufficiently mature to undertake such a responsibility. We are entirely dependent upon our mothers; they sustain us and keep us safe; they are the sources of love that bathe us in complete acceptance of who we are and give us the assurance of her presence whenever she is needed. Dependence is formed, and then a trust that we begin to look for in others outside the mother relationship, which we require for all life challenges.

The first year of a child's life is a struggle between trust and mistrust. Our experiences with our mothers or mother substitutes hinge on the formation of critical bonds, where the mother takes the responsibility for birthing and nurturing her child; the child, in turn, is totally dependent upon the mother for survival. Trust is the essential byproduct of this stage. If there is inconsistency or distraction in the mother's care for the baby, a lack of trust may be established, since the baby can't always count on the mother being there for safety and nurturing.

This dynamic is even present in the animal world, to a much lesser degree. A poignant story of a veterinarian perhaps demonstrates this concept in a very literal way. He found a fawn in a ditch, near its dead mother. He stopped and took the terrified deer to his home, making a safe place for it in his garage. He went to a feed store and got the proper substitutes to nurture it, and their relationship became like that between mother and child. As the fawn grew more stable and capable of independent actions, the vet left him in a nearby wooded area. In the mornings, he would whistle a signal familiar to the baby. The deer would come out of the woods, where his substitute mother would feed and comfort him. The fawn was spooked by other humans, so to observe this beautiful ritual it was necessary for the observer to hide out of sight from the deer. The fawn had instinctively "imprinted" with the vet from the beginning of their relationship. Eventually, the vet knew he had to change this relationship and wean the deer off its dependency on him. The compassionate veterinarian found it hard too, to extract himself from this bond, but knew the deer wouldn't survive unless he found a herd to join. Each day, the growing fawn came for less food, and the vet would watch it go further away from his artificial home, slowly gaining its independence.

In the animal kingdom, the growth period is luckily accelerated, so temporary motherhood worked out for the survival and adjustment of the fawn. The veterinarian thinks he sees him now and again at the edge of the woods.

In a human environment, the need for a mother to give prolonged care is imminent. The initial months of life are the most physically demanding, requiring a mother to be at hand nearly twenty four hours a day. This is grueling; ask any mother.

She has little sleep and is required to give unconditionally to the baby. She learns to interpret the types of cries a child broadcasts: I'm hungry; I'm soiled; I'm sick; I'm just not happy. Eventually the child starts to communicate his or her needs orally, but not without demands and crying. Mothers witness the epitome of immaturity in their children and must become their unrelenting guides, trying to lead them toward independence and maturity. It is a feverish, frustrating, and rewarding process that lasts until the child is in early adulthood.

If the mother manages to achieve a trusting relationship with her child throughout the maturation process, then the child will have the ability to transfer the trusting bond to other relationships, eventually trusting in the world and his or her future. If the mother–child experience is negative, the child will live with fear and suspicion, experiencing problems in forming future relationships throughout life. Because the consequences of the mother–child relationship are so critical, it is imperative that women understand their impending role before they become pregnant. This also means it is essential that the future mother have some modicum of maturity.

Being mature requires more than having a body that can reproduce. This ability to reproduce is indicative of physical maturity only; it points to a female who has reached menses and has the potential for motherhood. The maturity required for motherhood has a spiritual inflection. Her IHood must be capable of unconditional love; she must be consciously inclined in giving to the child rather than the receiving of any self-gratification. She must have the ability to be patient and acknowledge and understand that she alone, may have sole responsibility for this child to have a demeanor of mental and emotional presence.

Dear Annie, a syndicated advice column, recently headlined

"Jobless and Pregnant at Seventeen." We know this to be a potential disaster. We could dissect why this girl became pregnant, but this isn't the point. The consequence of her poor decision is bringing a life into her world, which may be forever blighted. It is a problem for both the baby and the pregnant youth. Can we honestly say that this teen's decision was anything but self-serving? She said she acquiesced in order to make her boyfriend feel happy because he had always wanted children. Would it be any more sensible if she became pregnant to keep her relationship with this boy by trapping him? It is all the same egoic, immature, clouded thinking. There is no evidence of maturity or preparedness to accept the immense responsibility this young woman has in front of her. Her divine nature is not in control yet, though it is present. The ego has inserted itself in the vilest of ways, perhaps destroying many lives.

Not to be ignored, there are women among us who, for all appearances, are ready for motherhood. They have planned their futures to include parenthood and they are excited for their children's arrivals. But once a child is born, the mother's life is so radically changed that she cannot accept her new role and at best, tolerates her situation. Many of us find ourselves along that long continuum between the perfect mother–child relationship and the toxic one. Though it is usually in the middle of these extremes that we find ourselves, we have all probably witnessed the tragedy and devastating effects of a toxic mother–child relationship. The ability of a child to cope in his world, as well as that of the mother, is significantly impaired. The mother is missing in action or inconsistent in the relationship. The child can't count on the mother, and therefore can't trust her to be there, no matter what. Without trust, the child has nobody to rely on. Eventually the malfunctioning relationship influences the outer ring of the child's social circle, where an innate lack of confidence develops.

The maturity of the mother is compromised in some way, resulting in a breach in the mother–child bond. The entrusted arrangement to "mother" a child is neglected and the child is left to survive, emotionally and perhaps physically. Is this child now doomed? I don't believe so. This is where spirit is truly the potential savior for our IHood existence.

We know the expression: "hope springs eternal in the human breast", from *An Essay on Man*[7] penned by Alexander Pope in the early 1700s.

> Where does this hope come from? It originates in our soul. It permeates our instinctive knowing; God assures us with this gift; we are not alone, no matter what the circumstance. The spiritual dimension of all of us has always existed, even though, as a child, it may not have been identified as such. It is the love in our hearts for our self and for any relationship where a bond is formed. It further expresses itself in an outer circle as we mature in our understanding and ability to recognize that giving love is the way to our purpose. Love is sourced from the well of our soul.

Furthermore, he continued:

> God loves from whole to parts: but human soul must rise from individual to the whole. Self-love but serves the virtuous mind to wake, as the small pebble stirs the peaceful lake; The centre mov'd,

---

7   Pope, An Essay on Man, 1732 - 1734

a circle straight succeeds, another still, and still another spreads; Friends, parent, neighbour, first it will embrace; his country next; and next all human race; wide and more wide, th' o'erflowings of the mind.

Take ev'ry creature in of ev'ry kind: Earth smiles around, with boundless bounty blest, And Heav'n beholds its image in his breast.

Circumstances befall all of us in our human state. It is not my purpose to point a finger at misguided or immature mothers. We put forth our best effort in our circumstances and at the moment of our decisions. We can agree that the outcomes are not always positive. A mother, when exhausted and at her wits end, is more easily pulled into her egoic thinking and more apt to do disservice to her child because of her inability to give any more in that moment. Whatever action she might have taken that was immature and self-serving will end up, no doubt, in her mind under the "guilt" column.

Guilt happens when we behave outside of our integrity. In order to succeed in this self-evaluation, we need to start by recognizing actions and behaviors that were not from our spiritually driven mind but rather our ego–self–body mind, and forgive ourselves. It is no more complicated than untangling a rope of knots. We can straighten out our thinking by detangling our thoughts and our intentions, recognize off target thinking and right ourselves. When we do this, we can transform the negative actions into positive solutions for the future.

We know the truthful direction to take. We must listen to our inner voice, the one that is pointing to the light. When similar circumstances present themselves, we need to be aware of our weakness and continue to overcome the urge to succumb to the selfish, egoic mind. God created time so that we could have plenty of it to learn our divine purpose in this earthly experience; time allows us to mature through discovering negative patterns that keep us in the ego. The basic drill follows like this:

1. Identify our reactive behavior (wrong thinking)
2. Examine the reasons for its repetition, the triggers
3. Move to consciously correct our behavior with help from introspection (our spirit) and achieve "right" thinking
4. Seek help if we can't move beyond the correction (It may be that you need outside assistance; i.e., another's helping hand or even professional help. It is right minded to recognize this too.)

This process is how we illuminate the rights and wrongs in our lives and work purposefully to maintain love based thinking.

Does this mean we are now sentenced to a life that must always be serious, self-sacrificing, and deep in thought during our entire wakefulness? Of course we aren't. We can be the life of the party! Be the joy of our own life! It happens when we finally identify the source of our immaturity and where our weaknesses lie; it usually stems from our total self-absorption. We can do some self-reflection on this point. The frequent examination of our ego habits can set us free and bring us more closely to understanding where we get tripped up.

Some questions we can ask ourselves are: "Are we always out of patience with our children (and people in general)?" "Why?" "What is more important to do that is pressing us?" "Do we constantly feel sorry for ourselves and all that we have to do, thinking nobody ever helps us?" Habits imply there is a pattern of behavior in the situations that arise. We aren't talking about the occasional self-pity party. It's when we choose to serve ourselves, frequently, over the needs of others; then we know it is the ego stepping up to the plate for the selfish intent of serving the "me," not the "others" in our lives. The immature pattern requires our attention to be transfigured through the help of spirit.

When we consciously make the effort to attack our human flaws as viruses, we find peace in our divine maturity, instead of the egoic, immature chaos in self. Let's face it; most of us are not doing the metaphorical big bad wolf stuff. We choose fibs and white lies, exaggerated truths. We cuss at people, and chastise and criticize our children without thinking. We all know the habits we perform with ugly regularity. They are demons that accumulate in the corners of our lives like dust bunnies under the bed. Eventually we will get sick of them. The revelation will come to us; perhaps in the form of our children repeating/reenacting them, and they will seem uglier and misplaced coming from their mouths.

We recognize how the lessons that we teach may not be coming from the source but from the ego. We see that we are reinforcing the very behaviors that keep us in our anger, guilt, and confusion; in our human turmoil. When we flip the switch to our "right" thinking, to our spiritual side of the IHood, then we can see and feel the change; and in the long run, so can humanity.

In our struggle to gain maturity, the spirit divine intervenes in our lives; otherwise, we would never have hope for our own futures. We might never have a "happy ending." We know that we all have souls, and therefore, hope. Relationships are based on acceptance and rejection; approval and disapproval: giving, taking and compromise. All of these are based on the existence of love. Love is at the very root of the reason to live. Love is the living verb;

the action required of us to express our divinity; the emotional evidence of our God given spirit. Without love in fact, we will die. In 1946, psychiatrist Rene Spitz reported on children in institutional settings and found that infants suffered from *tristeza* (sadness), caused by the lack of maternal love in a non-caring, institutional environment. The majority of those lucky enough to survive infancy suffered from psychiatric illness, blamed on the lack of maternal bonds in their young lives[8].

> Where does love come from? Is it innate in our physical body? No, it is divined in our spirit and is the essence of our existence. "You shall love the Lord your God with all your heart, and with all your soul, and with all your mind, and with all your strength .... You shall love your neighbor as yourself. There is no other commandment greater than these."
>
> (Mark 12:30-31 NKSV)

In the letter of Paul to the Galatians, the difference between our human body and our divine spirit is made clear, and again confirms the divine dimension of our maturity.

> "The works of the flesh [our purely human, ego driven existence] include impurity, licentiousness, idolatry, strife, jealousy, anger, selfishness, envy, drunkenness ... but the fruit of the spirit is love, joy, peace, patience, kindness, goodness, faithfulness, gentleness, and self-control ... let us have no

---

8   Spitz, *Psychoanalytic Study of the Child, 1946*

conceit, no provoking of one another, no envy of one another. "

(Galatians 5:19–23 RSV)

It's pretty clear; when it comes to maturity, we can see where one type of behavior leads to misery and chaos, and the other to calm and happiness. The obvious difference between the behaviors of ego and those of spirit is the love emotion that carries the spirit into action in our lives. It is love's presence, or lack of presence, that foretells the choices we make.

Hopefully we can see that a key ingredient in the success of achieving the trust bond between mother and child is the maturity of the mother, capable of unconditional love, and the mother's willingness to work toward achieving a more homeostatic relationship in her IHood, shunning the human inclination to be dominated by ego; embracing unconditional love for her child. This is a huge responsibility and not one to be taken lightly, as we recognize.

Second Year of Life: Parents, Responsibility, and Control

The prominent figures in a child's life expand now from mother and self to include the father. The child is aware of a larger world now. Since this relationship to the child fosters the ability to gain autonomy in his or her life, it is important to note certain variations to the "core" family. The nuclear family; defined by a father, mother, and child, has decreased in number in our present society. Is this change, which now includes more single parent units and extended family units, a healthy one? Is it more egoic than spiritual, considering the needs of children? One wonders about the influences of the family dynamic on today's children, and if it affects the success of children in reaching maturity and autonomy. There is not sufficient data to verify or negate the questions.

When it comes to studying human behavior, we have little more than observable behavior to draw assumptions from. Healthy parental relationships for children, no matter what the living arrangements happen to be, have been proven to be of the utmost importance. The quality of the relationships seems to be based upon the love children receive from key people in their lives.

Other factors in the relationship are expectations parents have for their maturing child. There needs to be nurturing, non-threatening environments where a baby begins to explore his or her world and can gain success on his or her own volition. For example, learning how to walk, talk, feed him or herself, choose toys to play with, and co-play with others. It is also during this time when the parents can assert their expectations of the beginning phase of self-control, as well as self-restraint. These skills are acquired with the help of parental guidance, leading to the beginning of a child's ability to experience self-esteem through success in accomplishing these tasks.

It may seem improbable to have an expectation of self-control and self-restraint at the tender age of two years old. But in fact, this is when a child is ideally suited to take limited responsibility for his or her actions. This phase need not be physically punitive. For example, if a child has been playing with blocks and then leaves the activity for another, it is the expectation of the parents that the child put the toys away. If at first the child resists that responsibility, all a parent needs to do is acknowledge the resistance and ask again for his or her help. If the child refuses, the parent picks up the blocks and puts them away. The next time the child wishes to play with the blocks, the parent does not make them accessible. When the child wishes to play with them again, the parent explains that there is an expectation that the child will willingly pick up the blocks. The child will get the idea after a few reminders.

For whatever reason, it seems that parents resist teaching responsibility to their youngsters. It may be that it requires more patience and maturity on the parents' part than they are willing to give. The consequence is that parents seem to postpone, or worse, totally ignore, this important aspect of childhood responsibility. It really doesn't make much logical sense, since it is better to gain responsibility earlier, when children learn to contribute to the family and begin to gain self-control. Otherwise, if children are denied opportunities to learn about the positive outcomes of cooperation and taking responsibility for their play, the parents will begin to struggle with control issues with their children. The consequence is that parents feel disappointed in their children's lack of cooperation, no doubt expressing it toward them; children, on the other hand, begin to believe they are entitled to having parents do their work, becoming resentful when anything is asked of them.

Parents are caregivers with huge responsibilities. Stable, firm, and loving guidance is part of the process of child rearing in order for children to achieve maturity. Children need to learn that we all have on going responsibilities. Responsibility needs to be seen as a normal course of events in everyday life. It is part of maturation. Without this understanding, we miss opportunities for our children to grow into productive adults. Though it may be difficult, parents need to teach their children responsibility in small doses so resentment isn't a byproduct of the relationship.

Somehow, it may be construed as more fun for our offspring to have less responsibility. But since when have fun and responsibility become opposites? It may be that parents had a tough burdensome childhood, so they see their opportunity to give their children something better. Taking responsibility however, is the key ingredient in ultimate happiness and independence. It is a moment of prideful accomplishment when a child completes a task for the first time and sees his or her role in the family as a contributor. The prevailing attitude of avoidance of responsibility for children is perhaps the biggest disservice we can dish out as parents. Our society is seeing the fallout of such practices.

Many children and young adults are becoming ships without rudders; their great potentials put on hold. They are adrift with misconceptions of how the world should work, seeing responsibility as a bad thing, rather than the barometer for their successful acquisition of maturity. Parents need to change their perception of responsibility as well, understanding that it is a key ingredient in acquiring our developmental skills and seeking our purpose on this earth. It begins with small steps.

> To everything there is a season, a time to sow and
> a time to reap; a time to seek and a time to lose; a
> time to break down and a time to build up.
>
> (Ecclesiastes 3: 1-3)

As parents, we need to take the readiness of our children and turn it into fruitful opportunities for their growth. It is through the attitudes of parents that children build their attitudes as well. Parents are the models. The praise that a child receives as "Daddy's little helper" is important to the self-esteem of the child. It is beneficial to the positive attitudes that will be formulated about present and future responsibilities.

There is a phrase we have all probably heard in our lifetime, "Everything in moderation." When parents start to dish out tasks to their children, they should remember this phrase. If the task is not age appropriate, it will be too much to expect and will probably result in a negative outcome.

Parents may have motivations that do not serve their children's best interests. There are those who have an inclination to keep children in a state of being "too young" (irresponsible) for too long. Some may be laissez faire and not bother to follow through on any expectations of their children. Then there are those who shovel off to their children whatever it is that they do not want to do. If parents wish to check what their motivations are when dealing with their children, the test may be to ask, "Who is benefiting from my demands for certain expected behavior?" Is it for my child, in the long run, or for me?

There are negative outcomes in this age group, which include the potential of a sense of loss of control of one's internal and external world, a propensity for shame, and doubt about personal control in general. If you think about how to combat these outcomes, it becomes fairly obvious that lack of responsibility in children's lives is indeed a culprit that can lead to these developmental shortcomings.

Self-worth is the payoff for learning to take responsibility for ourselves. It begins at the smallest acknowledgment, mutually recognized as children begin to see themselves as separate from their parents. The hair of a root finds the soil; the seed takes the nutrition after its first sprout; children celebrate their first steps with the joyful applause of their parents.

There are "markers" for expressing independence. The two year old's mantra, "mine," sends the message of discovering one's own entity and identity. It is now that the opportunity for parents to create the teachable moment occurs. Encouragement to walk is one of the first signals for the child to take responsibility for his mobility; it is the initial independence taken by him alone. Children differ developmentally, with some more ready for independence than others. Encourage independent and responsible actions and applaud when they occur. Self-worth is the end game here. Shame results when children are allowed to avoid a task they don't want to do, even when they know they are capable. They begin to understand that they have the power and that they are not honoring their mothers and fathers. The slippery slope of parental loss of control begins, and children feel shame. It is much more simple and direct to be clear with parental expectations; explain the consequences of non-compliance, and follow through. A non-threatening, firm disciplinary approach leads to great benefit for all.

Reader Reflections

9
Spiritual Awareness
Age Three through Age Nine

Family and Confidence

IT IS WITH GREAT pleasure that I relate a story from an experience with my then three year old granddaughter, Ella. It was during a visit when my daughter mentioned she was concerned with Ella because she would say, on occasion, that she "wanted to go home," even though she was in her own home. I asked my daughter if I could ask Ella about this, since I had always felt she was a very spiritual child, perhaps an Indigo,[9] for quite some time. She made the same comment about wanting to go home while we were together on their back deck.

I sat beside Ella, and asked her where home was. She answered very directly by pointing up to the sky, saying, "Up there, Grandma."

"Do you mean up in heaven, Ella?" I asked.

"Yes." She answered.

"Who lives there, Ella?" I inquired.

"You do, Grandma."

A bit confused, I went on. "Who else lives there, Ella?"

---

9   Carroll and Tober, *The Indigo Children: The New Kids Have Arrived*, 1999.

"Me," she answered. Then she went on, "Ask me who else lives there, Grandma."

I did ask her. She replied, "Grandpa. Ask me who else."

Not to be daunted, I then asked her what heaven looked like. She told me, "It's beautiful, with all the colors of the rainbow." I asked her if God was there.

She looked at me and laughed. "Yes … you know that!"

Then she walked away to play with her brother. These children feel a connection with God and heaven.

To me, the conversation suggested that Ella was certainly hardwired with the magnificence of spirit. Others might say that Ella is precocious, a typical dramatic, exaggerated three year old. Hearing Ella's descriptions, I believe there was truth in what she said. There is essential needs satisfaction required as Ella matures; a positive love connection, positive examples from parents and friends, and self-love. Without them she will have difficulty evolving fully with a spiritual connection.

It is in this stage that children must convince themselves that they are real people, and want to know what kind of person each is going to be. The complete family that surrounds them now influences children. They are very observant of others' behavior; this is why the model behavior of parents is essential. Children begin to copy what they see their parents do, as well as their siblings.

Parent responsibility continues to be demanding now. When setting an example for our children, the questions for parents become, "Which example are we: positive or negative; consistent or inconsistent? Do our children observe behavior that says 'Do as I say, not as I do'?" It is inevitable that parents are a mixed bag of their own egoic needs, and at the same time selfless in tending their children. Mature parents try to be a positive example as much as possible. This is the time when the "cursing" habit may get curtailed; smoking habits may end; poor table manners turn into good ones. These parents understand the incredible impact they have on their children's lives and persevere in their responsibility to teach them about life. They want their offspring to become loving contributors to family life; to learn to be givers, not just takers. Children, believe it or not, want this outcome too. They enjoy responsibility. They want to feel the reward of giving and contributing, of being relied upon. These responsibilities need to be modeled and lovingly taught.

There was a working mom who never asked anything of her children. When she came home, she did everything: made the dinner, set the table, picked up carelessly discarded bikes in the driveway; all the daily chores of life. As the children grew, they grew to expect things of their mother. One day she found she had a physical problem that required surgery with a lengthy recovery. Her husband was overcome by the responsibilities left to him, and the children were oblivious to the needs of either parent. There was little compassion for their mother or father's situation, since they had neither the recognition of their parents' sacrifice, nor the experience of working with and contributing to the family.

If we are without proper guidance and loving lessons, which teach about the responsibilities of family membership, the joy of helping, and the significance of commitment, then we may not release our selfish existence. We may find ourselves stuck in the perpetual state of entitlement. It is only through family obligations and performing acts of kindness and generosity to others that we find true love, true happiness, and true peace. While it may seem that ages three through nine are very young to start this process, it is indeed appropriate.

When small children begin to mimic their parents by taking

dishes to the sink, or donning an apron and dusting in the house, it is tempting to pat them on the head and tell them how "cute" they are, and nothing more. This is actually an opportunity for parents to encourage the continued behavior of such actions and use the moment to tell children how much they appreciate them. Believe it or not, these small acts have a serious impact on this age group, especially in this phase of their ego development. Children take their helpful actions seriously, so it is inappropriate to minimize this behavior, since they may construe this as belittling.

Children have anxieties and conflicts that always need to be treated with respect. Through acceptance of the real and imagined play of children, adults confirm the authenticity of their children's existence, allowing them to become more confident in their budding roles as people. Children exhibit their newfound confidence by embarking beyond their old limitations and exploring the physical world around them, sometimes with alarming inquisitiveness and perhaps dangerous behavior. Parents need to inject the balance of reality and safety, which immature children do not understand in these explorations. It is not an easy phase of development for anyone in the family, since it is critical to not overly restrict children.

Another marker of this stage of development is the development of conscience. Children become independent and self-reliant, and can be trusted to recognize family traditions and values. It is also the time that children "normally" can exhibit cruel, unsocial behavior. Parents need to recognize their children are not evil, but rather uninhibited. It doesn't mean that parents should ignore the behavior; nor does it mean they should overreact to it. Again, it requires a mature, loving response of moderation on the part of the parents.

A potential issue for children of this age group is parental expectation. We are all too familiar with our faults and don't want to see them repeated in our children's behavior. The mixed messages that we send are confusing and may result in deep conflicts within children. Parents may be seen as an unjust power trying to suppress a child's desires. Parents need to analyze if the behavior they are teaching is for the good of the children or for themselves. This is also an opportune time for parents to do self-reflection, checking to see if they are asking for more from their children than they exemplify themselves.

The hope is that children at this stage will escape the dominant feeling of fear of punishment by their adult influencers. An indication of this negative outcome may be excessive showing off. If parents see a dominance of appearance in these behaviors, it is a cue to reflect upon their own personal actions.

In the development of conscience, we see the onset of guilt during this stage of life. This is a cautious time. There is a man I know who tells of when he was six years old. He was visiting his sick uncle, who decided to roughhouse with him. A few days after his visit, the uncle died. His mother told him it was probably because he was too rough with his uncle. This man still suffers the guilt of this action, and he is in his seventies. He says, "It's not my fault," when things go wrong. This painful existence should never have occurred in his life. His mother, no doubt, was suffering herself with the thought that her son might have overtaxed her brother; but it was unimaginable that she made the comment to her son.

Because of guilt burdened lives, many adults feel that their worth as people consists entirely of what they are doing or what they are going to do next and not their value as individuals. The negative consequences of guilt can ruin lives.

The more positive result of the formation of conscience and guilt is that children become more responsible and self-disciplined with their behavior. Parents need to strive toward a balance in their children's development, between encouraging self-control and the constant need to badger what is seen as misbehavior.

This age group begins viewing "others" from an entirely new perspective; they start to understand that existence on earth is not solely for personal pleasure. This monumental event in development opens the door to self-revelation, the impact of personal choices as well as an internal dialogue involving free choice. This time frame offers an unlimited opportunity for the appearance of non-selfish behavior.

It is not surprising in this age group then, that we begin to embrace the notion that parents and society in general need to acknowledge this period as a "coming of age", to officially welcome and encourage children to grow up, take further responsibility for developing their God given gifts, and expand spiritual growth in particular.

Many religious faiths have formal ceremonies, emphasizing personal accountability from various traditions. Christians believe that children are capable of accepting moral responsibility between the ages of seven and twelve, depending upon the differences between personal and psychological maturation. Some children are allowed to receive Holy Communion within their church between the ages of eight and nine, after instruction of the sacrament of penance, whereby children come to understand the traditional rite. The rite includes showing remorse for particular wrongful actions; the examination of conscience and disclosing any wrongdoing to a priest in confession, absolution through penance (requiring children to redeem themselves by doing something that makes up for their sins). Christians believe that confessing wrongful thinking and actions to a priest, or in silence before a congregation and God, will lead children toward the full development of conscience.

Other religious beliefs use confession as well. Buddhists confess to a superior in the temple; Jews seek forgiveness from God and not through man, as do those who believe in Muhammad. In Eastern Orthodoxy, confession and repentance has less to do with a child returning to a "pure" state than with individual spiritual development. Much responsibility is given to this age group, believing that children can be trusted to formulate their own spiritual life.

Certain obligations may be foisted upon this age group as they reach the age of moral responsibility. Christians may now be able to assist at Sunday Mass, attend holy days, abstain from meat, and participate in annual penance services. They may also be eligible to sponsor a child at baptism or witness a marriage.

In Islam, children are not required to perform any acts of Sharia before they reach puberty. Once physical characteristics change, they are required to perform certain prayers and obligations.

With Judaism, girls become of age at their twelfth year, celebrating their bat mitzvah; boys celebrate at the age of thirteen with a bar mitzvah. Much preparation is required for these serious hallmarks, including religious instruction for several years.

Adult Hindus make a decision as to when a child has matured enough to understand his or her responsibility to family and society. The child then celebrates this decision by participating in a ceremony. Females dress in a sari and are then acknowledged by their community. For boys, there is a sacred thread ceremony for Dvija (twice born).

Another demonstration of gained maturity appears in the form of enjoyment when producing something. The bloom of this mature thinking begins to compete with free time spent in idle play. This development of productivity comes with the need for esteem that accompanies accomplishment and pride.

Despite all of the celebrations and productivity associated with this age, what evolves is not a stronger belief system, but rather a malaise in the United States. Though the teachings of morality and responsibility seem to be clearly encouraged and understood by children, there appears to be a discontinuation of religious study once the ceremonies are over. It seems that after the celebration ends, there is little evidence of practiced faith, or expectation of it.

The problem lies with the execution of continued practice by parents. For whatever reason, the adult population in this country is falling away from formal religious practices. Children who have reached the moral understanding, and celebrate through traditional ceremonies, are not supported by parental example thereafter. Parents become less enthusiastic in their encouragement of the very tenets they just celebrated, much to the bewilderment of the new celebrants. Many are doing no more than going through the motions of propriety and shirking the actual commitment to their beliefs.

In contrast, parents continue to applaud the productive worldly elements of their children's development, encouraging school accomplishments and giving more responsibility to their lives. Is it any wonder that many children find this confounding? When parents depart from their responsibility of spiritual training, honing in on only the worldly training of their children, it's no wonder children lose sight of their spiritual compass. Often, children become cynical of adult behavior and as a result, question the very essence of the world's belief system. It seems easier to be fully operational in our three dimensional, physical world, choosing what is physically satisfying. In doing so, we depart from the right thinking of spiritual recognition in our IHood.

For this very reason, we find this age of social development to be a glaringly thwarted period, threatening us from fully capturing our maturity. Society in general and parents in particular, find it acceptable to turn their heads the other way when their children begin to abandon fundamental beliefs that keep them in truth and integrity. Parents willingly participate, watching their children openly choose wrong thinking, blaming it on "a phase they're going through" or peer pressure.

It is true that this age group identifies more and more with their friends than with family. It is a natural phenomenon. But this is also the time in which they develop character and an ability to garner inner strength to refrain from making decisions they know to be wrong. There is an epidemic of pubescent children fully engaged in pursuits of alcohol, drugs, and sexual experimentation, and it did not happen overnight.

Parents and the adult community are the proper focus to examine what is truly happening to teens. What is "reasonable" behavior for this age? When does responsibility for one's own behavior begin? Who is responsible for enlightening them? These are complicated questions that will be addressed in the next chapter. We must begin when children are young and observe their response to their own abilities. Are they exhibiting maturity in their choices? Do they have enough freedom to experiment in these choices, or do parents have a death grip on every move they make, encouraging them to behave differently when they are not under their parents' thumbs?

It is my belief that we are abandoning youth who choose without morals. It is an adult epidemic, underscored by cowardice to follow through with what is right minded thinking. This right minded thinking is what leads the way out of chaos and into peaceful life practices. When children do not take responsibility, they are not responding to their abilities. When parents allow them to choose to turn their backs on the abilities they have been given by God, they are taking them for granted and not giving them value. It is like throwing away gifts, except much more devastating, since these come from our Creator and are the markers that make us unique on earth.

The gifts that characterize us are the foundation for our fundamental dignity. They are the touchstone of truth, integrity, and happiness. Though our human life has physical boundaries, these human gifts allow us to see our spirit source as well. In these natural ways, we come to know God.

Reader Reflections

10
Spiritual Integration
Adolescence and Puberty

Physical, Emotional, and Spiritual Challenges

PUBERTY AND ADOLESCENCE FORM another challenging growth period in our human development. All of us have memories of awkwardness and insecurities. The transition from childhood to adulthood is fraught with challenges: physical, emotional, and spiritual. It's like having one foot in a slow moving boat and the other on a dock. Often our indecision causes us to fall into the water.

At this time, our spirit potentially integrates within our daily routine. Not only are we ready to understand and acknowledge our spiritual existence, we can begin to commit to more right minded decisions. As we proceed in our maturity, we see the larger picture of how our world operates. We make choices that are influenced by prior experiences and peer activity. If we are associating with friends who are striving toward academic achievement, involved in a variety of sports and practicing ethical behavior, then we are inclined to behave in a similar manner. If we are exposed to the obvious bad choices made by friends and acquaintances (teen pregnancy, drug usage, truancy, gang improprieties), then we make conscious internal decisions about how we might react in those circumstances. Our perception of these situations is usually a result of how our maturity cycle has been running up to this point. If we are unable to resist remarkably bad decisions, then we are going to have more than our share of chaos and misery.

Most obvious is the presence of extreme physical changes. Children who were shorter than their mothers six months ago, are suddenly the same height or taller. There are "spurts" where growth seems to occur overnight. There is literally an aching of bones and muscles resulting from rapid growth during adolescence. Appetites increase, and acne may become a normal but confounding reminder that hormones of a different type are entering and taking control of this newly forming body. Girls complain that they are taller than the boys in their class, causing consternation and fear that they will stand out in their awkwardness. Boys fear they will be stalled in their growth. Weight becomes an issue for both sexes as well. In a society of fast food, the marginalization of "normal" weight may occur. Those who are unduly reminded of their heft may experience eating disorders, choosing to overeat, become bulimic or anorexic, or any one of a number of options to stay in control of their bodies.

Changes during adolescence exacerbate any stressful situation, causing an emotional rollercoaster for these soon to be adults. There are esteem issues, especially when a teen can't seem to find an aptitude with which he excels, and he wants to excel at everything.

Many adults who witness emotional reactions of teens often judge them critically since traditionally, we see those governed by emotion as lacking in reason or willpower. Our reaction to situations is a choice we make. It is a time influenced by cliques and social pressures. Teens often find themselves chastised by others or engaged in bullying behavior. There is positioning for popularity. Everybody wants to belong. There may be an "I'm better than you" attitude prevailing in the group. Little empathy is expressed for peers who are being victimized. It is a time where teens must confront the issue of "What's in it for me?"

Middle schools populated with this age group have an opportunity to help students during this rough time, but their resources are often limited. There is a promising program from Toronto, Canada, called "Roots of Empathy: Changing the World Child by Child"[10] which shows great promise to help teens become better adjusted. Mary Gordon, the founder, allows students the opportunity to observe two parents and a small child, who come to their classroom. Adults and children problem solve together, helping the students to internalize their own vision of family and love. The goal is to have students move to a caring school community. They shift from negative agendas of communication to positive ones. Students observe and interact with the family throughout the seventh and eighth grades. Many lessons are learned about the worth of human beings, children's physical and emotional needs, how to recognize an array of emotional expression, and the difficulty of being a parent. The promise of this program is that teens can learn to read emotional reaction and open the door to their own feelings, appreciating those of others as well. This is a giant step toward maturity. It has multiple outcomes, including demonstrating how the baby comes first, and witnessing the economic responsibilities of parents. It is interesting to note that this program has resulted in fewer teen pregnancies.

Decision making is more of a prominent skill for teens. They need plenty of practice with the less important decisions so they

---

10   www.rootsofempathy.org

can evolve to the ones to be made at this stage. A word of caution for parents: when children are overly directed and not allowed to make even the most trivial decision it prevents them from being able to make smaller decisions independent of your guidance. They will feel the need to check with authority about everything; they will not have confidence in their judgment. This can lead to further issues when they are given freedom to decide. They may indeed "fail" when they are given full choice in the school cafeteria, choosing less than nutritious foods that they now can personally choose without criticism. They may start dressing in "comfortable" clothes, rather than those deemed appropriate by their parents. Their individual choices may seem contrary to past expectations and behaviors. The extremes are more pronounced in cases where children were limited for too long; they were developmentally ready to make this level of decision earlier, but parental trust of their ability to do so was limited.

Ideally, parents recognize when to let loose of control as children demonstrate maturity and can take on their next journey in responsibility. If a child makes a poor decision, the privilege of choice is removed, a teaching/learning period is injected, and after an appropriate time, the child again is given free choice. We know that this is not a perfect scenario, with many of us stopping and starting inappropriately and indiscriminately. When children are given too much responsibility prematurely for their development, they fail, and are subject to condemnation for their actions. Conversely, many are not given any responsibility or trust, resulting in inexperience and perhaps out of control behavior when they finally are given the chance. We have an imperfect science here.

It is not surprising that we overlook our children's spiritual development amid this chaos. The combination of maturity and recognition of our spirituality (part of IHood) can transform the chaos of these years into a more peaceful existence. It is important, then, for parents to inject ethical and moral discussion into family life.

When children are familiarized of their spirituality, they do not question it because they know it to be true from their past collective consciousness; it is in their belief system. It is a natural state of knowing, like their physical presence. Thus, when children are given the challenges of taking responsibility, acquainted with abilities, and trusted to make decisions when they are able to do so, they have comfort, both physically and spiritually that they are emotionally stable and progressing toward a path of purpose.

When puberty and adolescence are conflicted, we see independent teens teetering between the yearnings for the safety of family and the company of peers, seeking parties, but also seeking parental counsel and behavioral acceptance. It is not surprising to find this to be a time when parents wring their hands, hoping the groundwork they laid during pre-pubescence created enough of an impact to keep their children out of trouble.

Depending upon the degree to which a teen has gained maturity at this phase of development, parents may witness their children abandoning belief systems that once aligned with that of the family, often trying out rebellious behaviors that they never took up in the past. Though initially happy in earlier years, teens may become more sensitive and moody. They may exhibit a desire to spend more time alone in their rooms. They seek television, Game Boys, Wii and all forms of electronic games. They beg for electronics that will keep them in touch with their friends, and will use social networks.

Ironically, despite seeming to want complete independence, teens really want their parents' time, love, attention, and approval.

They are in a period of complete unpredictability and confusion. It is a time that calls parents to rally to our children's sides and to be patient, exhibiting all the parental maturity we can muster in these challenging times.

The Sex Drive

It is during these stress filled years that another physical need of significant influence kicks into high gear: the sex drive. There are so many approaches to handling this almost impossible to control biological hunger that a book could easily be filled on it alone. Parents dread it; teens are excited and wary at the same time. There are discussions of morality, social responsibility, peer pressure, safe sex, birth control; the list goes on. Some teens are more prepared for the onslaught than others are.

Parents seem to have personal slants on how the subject should be approached, depending on their cultural and religious views. The local public or parochial schools have educational classes sanctioned by school boards or mandated by the state departments of education, which parents may or may not embrace. The attitudes, mores, and cultures that influence the education of teens vary from extremely permissive viewpoints, toward participation in sexual activity or extremely restrictive abstinence, allowing at most, a kiss and perhaps a hug that do not result in impure thoughts.

It is no wonder teens are totally confused, they are being pulled with urgency to follow their biological needs. It is a time when spiritual integration plays a strong role in our IHood. Teens hear typical arguments for permissive sexual behavior: "everybody's doing it," "it's no big deal if you use a condom," and so on. But they may find that they have a clearer understanding of what their true position is on this matter when discussing it with a knowledgeable parent.

There is no doubt about the peer pressure that persists. Oral sex, which some view as not actual sex, seems to be alive and well on school buses and under stairwells with onlookers. Dating a serious partner somehow allows for full sexual participation. All the time, these activities, which use to be reserved for experimenting college students, are drifting down into high school, and now middle schools or fifth and sixth graders. The parents and school officials who see the outbreak of teen pregnancies and of sexually transmitted diseases are appalled and fearful for their children.

Unfortunately, because of these fears and the lack of trust in their children's ability to resist sexual activity, parents and caregivers buy into the notion that their only solution to this phenomenon is to give teens birth control pills and condoms. They add side discussions about how kids their age should not be doing anything that necessitates use of prophylactics, but qualify it by saying, "if you are in a difficult situation, use good judgment." Thus, we see the dilemma form, a mixed message of satisfying a moral commitment versus a physical need.

It seems more responsible for the adult community to entertain a different line of thinking with their children. When we think of the emotional trauma and potential physical damage that our children are experiencing in this physically active sexual climate, it is no wonder children are confused. With peer pressure, they are risking self-respect issues and loss of self-esteem. Their bodies are experiencing a sexual instinct that is natural and demanding. Teens are being challenged to find their truth more now than at any other time in their lives. It is now that full spiritual integration is needed.

This is the first full-fledged test between the ego-body wanting fulfillment, and the spirit-soul pressing for a more desirable outcome. When we feel dominated by physical desires, our IHood is called upon to provide us with the self-restraint like never before. Freud and Maslow have discussed the physical craving for sex as being a basic need. So to put our IHood to the test by asking it to choose the more mature, spiritual response to a call for physical action is indeed a challenge. The key component to this struggle, however, is the recognition of what is truth.

In a rational, non-physical discussion, we know that teens are not prepared to be parents. Then why not use birth control? This is the next logical question to be raised. For one, the assumption is that teens do not have the fortitude or ability to resist the physical, sexual act. This is not true.

The second question that this now begs is, "What's the difference?" "Who is hurt by this form of entertainment and sexual pleasure?" A parent can list a multitude of answers, including "You're not ready for this yet." We also know there is the potential for remorse for those of religious persuasion who have strayed from their convictions.

The third reason is what I feel to be the most logical and persuasive choice a teen can understand for restraining from sexual exploits as an adolescent: Sexual restraint should be the test that we use to find our intended mate. It is the fruit of a covenant we make with another human to deny the tiger of physicality by using spiritual choice in the aspiration of chastity as a choice reflective of one's truth. If teens do not recognize they are capable of this, then they have not reached an understanding of their self-worth; they will feel a predilection to cave to temptation, thinking they can't resist it. It is an absolute priority to educate our children to realize that their obligation to self and integrity is of much more value than pleasing or serving the physical needs of peers.

If we were not successful in finding the person with whom we feel the depth of love that proposes the possibility of marriage, then why would we grant them access to our body? Coercion and coaxing are tempting but resistible. Being an independent thinker is admirable. Our body is our body. It is not loaned out for the pleasure of others. It is under our control. When we find a person we think we can truly love in physical and nonphysical ways, we propose an agreement to that person; we commit to each other and test the genuine ability to use self-restraint; a restraint from intimacy. Why? If two people can be in love and avoid intercourse, that says we are willing to give up other temptations in life as we go through adulthood. It speaks volumes about the character and truthfulness of the other. If we can overcome a physical desire that is said to be the strongest need in our life, then the husband can overcome the temptation of the cute gal in the bar when he's traveling; the wife can turn down an advance during a difficult time in a marriage. That is how maturity works. That is how self-denial works. We are the winners, because we know our truths and live them.

Is it possible that we cannot overcome the sexual needs of our adolescence? Of course it is. We may not have matured enough to understand the power of this drive and the consequences of poor decisions. Just like an alcoholic or drug abuser, we are human in our choices, and it is probable that our lack of maturity limited us in our understanding that we are capable of living a responsible, peaceful existence with individual freedom of choice. We are able to be free of peer pressure by using our free will. We commit to a better personal life, knowing that we are living in integrity.

Recognizing Abilities

Puberty and adolescence are times in which our abilities and lack thereof become more pronounced. Certain school subjects may be easier than others, reflecting intellectual prowess. Tests in middle school help indicate academic potential as well. Then the questions become, "Are we motivated to perform well in all our ability areas? What if we just don't care?"

What causes lack of motivation? Often it's peer pressure. For whatever reason, there is definite evidence that positive school performance is not accepted in some groups. Students sometimes physically abuse their peers for doing well. A student may be rebellious, conveying a message of "I don't care!" or "You can't make me!" to their parents. Unfortunately, the teen thinks that their behavior will punish their parents, when they are really denying themselves an innate potential.

Whatever the reason for non-performance, as long as students have the intelligence to do average to exemplary work, they need to recognize their potential and work toward honoring the gifts they have through performance. Parents know their children's capabilities. Those who are not able to have academic success can certainly find other skill areas that allow them to achieve potential. There are many alternative curriculums available through high school and apprenticeship programs. What matters is that we are each productive and that we find our life's work.

Deepak Chopra wrote about his children's education in his marvelous book *The Seven Spiritual Laws of Success*[11]. He told each of his children there was a reason they were in this life, and they had to find out the reason by themselves. From the age of four, they heard this, and he taught them how to meditate. He also said he never wanted them to worry about making a living; if they were unable to make a living he would provide for them. Further, he said not to focus on doing well in school, making the best grades, or going to the best colleges. Deepak told them, "What I really

11   Amber-Allen Publishing, 1994

want you to focus on is how you can serve humanity, and what your unique talents are." As a result of following their father's advice, they got the best grades and attended the best colleges, becoming financially self-sufficient in the process.

I wonder if I could have been that wise, brave, and trusting when my children were in school. Intellectually and spiritually, I think it makes more sense than anything we could do to encourage our children in this world. Realistically, it is probably difficult to promise that we will care for them if we all know it may not be possible. Nonetheless, we could still challenge our children to find their gifts from the time they are very young.

As teens progress into adulthood, it is the hope that spiritual integration strengthens and they can become independent, avoid negative peer influence, appreciate others for their talents and skills, have empathy for those unable or unwilling to take responsibility for obligations to others and to self, and recognize right minded and wrong minded decisions and their consequences.

Reader Reflections

11
Spiritual Synthesis
Adulthood through Middle Age

ADULTHOOD IS THE TIME for us to focus on the question, "Where are we going?" Postponing this decision is not an option. The assumption is that by adulthood we have acquired the maturity and motivation required to steadfastly be on our path of purpose, or at least on the way to it. We imprint our spiritual identity upon our talents, treasures, and abilities, expressing the package of who we are, and enact a plan of direction. Our skills may be similar to millions of other people, but we must remember that we are unique in our expression of them; we are one of a kind in our physical–spiritual being. We have a purpose that only we can fulfill. It is our challenge to arrange our life, collect our potential, and design a way to complete our divine mission.

Preferred Partners, Love, and Loyalty

As we attain chronological adulthood, we recognize that this is when we find our mates; we commit to a relationship and promise loyalty to our partner. During these years, we also seriously examine the path we are meant to follow in this world. This is the time when significant decisions are made. It is almost a "which came first, the chicken or the egg?" scenario. In choosing our life companion, we are heavily influenced by the purpose assigned to us as well. In *A Course in Miracles*[12] the question is asked, "Do I want to know my Father's will for me?" This is a significant question, since it pertains to integrating our worldly goals with our life's spiritual mission. We need to have sufficient maturity to acknowledge that there is a larger purpose for our life than that we have sought in the past; it is the time to take the responsibility to be an active instrument of love in our life; to make the critical difference intended for us to make during our lifetime.

If we choose a partner who does not share our values and beliefs, then we are choosing a life of struggle that may inhibit personal manifestation. The folly of marrying with only physical attraction and romantic love as its base is clear. We potentially will have different goals, needs, and desires. The most difficult union would be that of someone who is spiritually unconscious with someone who is awakened and conscious of their purpose. Each partner seeks to change the other. There is doubtful outcome of a happy ending.

The power of our life's path is also intertwined with that of our fellow humans. It is part of creation's plan. It keeps us united in purpose, especially when we extend our love to every life we touch. It helps us recognize that the intent for having a body is to serve God and humanity in the way He intended. The commitment to our purpose increases the joy of our Creator.

It is important to acknowledge that many of us have great difficulty embracing this concept of living our purpose. When we came into this world, we were conscious only of our physical

---

12 2007, Foundation for Inner Peace

needs, thus deeming us unconscious for a long time. If we did not mature to the point of being motivated to give *and* receive, then we will not awaken to our spirituality as the most significant part of our identity. Our challenge in life is to make right minded decisions when our jobs and physical needs are tugging at us. Our challenge in life is our test of free will, to choose primarily the needs of the ego or to serve the needs of another with our spirit.

It is mature and necessary to take care of our responsibilities in our physical world; we have made commitments. Indeed, we have prepared ourselves for obligations through education and the development of our abilities and unique talents to arrive at adulthood. These were the gifts given at birth to help us accomplish the tasks ahead. But the warning flag that must go up reminds us that these physical and mental accomplishments are not meant to serve our bodies and their comforts to the exclusion of our real reason to be here.

We tend to place too much faith in our body as our source of strength, rather than our spirit. How often do we find ourselves making plans that include satisfying our physical needs only? We use our body as the end, rather than the means. We create a cycle of self-serving saturation, constantly seeking the next self-gratification. The challenge that confronts us puts us in danger of becoming misaligned with our spiritual work. We need to remember that our life's path is not solely physical or spiritual, but rather the blending of our skills and abilities with the intent of fulfilling our service to God. This is when we become an instrument of love; we complete the puzzle piece of our human mission. This can be done while living in our physical world; that is the challenge.

When we commit to offering our love, living in integrity,

truth, and values, we are more easily in tune to live our purpose. Again, this does not necessitate a choice between our physical and spiritual existences. We live our ethical life in all aspects: family, friends, and business. Our spirit and body are always with us. In our IHood, we choose to honor our spiritual behavior over that of our body, that's all. Our bodies will not suffer from our mission. Remember, we are never "out" of our bodies while on earth, so we will always be in direct care of them. It's just that we seek to be less aware of our "needy" bodies as we mature and live in adulthood.

Even though we are given many gifts to manage our lives, we find we are sometimes lacking because we have never been exposed to a particular set of circumstances. This is never more evident than when we find a life partner and choose to have a family. Because this is much more than a biological event, we need a whole set of skills we never anticipated: changing diapers, bathing a slippery little body, feeding a moving target, diagnosing the reason for a cry. We give up late nights out and find that, perhaps for the first time in our lives, we are totally responsible for another human being. Parenthood is complicated, but if the parents are mature, they will be fast learners.

The step into parenthood is one of the most difficult transformations one can experience. It requires putting a child's needs above one's own. We must feed babies all through the night and cuddle them despite our exhaustion. One of the truest tests of consciousness we undergo is placing the demands of our physical well-being behind to that of another. It is an opportunity for our spiritual behavior to demonstrate unconditional love for children.

Parent or not, as we continue to develop through our experiences and base of knowledge, we branch out and try other venues that seem to be the direction we are seeking. We discover our "core"; we discover who we become; we evolve. We recognize what we have created and accept that which we have not; we become comfortable with our gifts and strengths. We know our weaknesses and fears; we are able to handle adversity and challenges. Some of us may make choices and decisions that keep us unconscious to our IHood; living in fear and chaos created by ego-based needs. These choices keep us in a world that denies spirit by not acknowledging its importance, or perhaps even its existence. In this choosing, one values things and ideas that are transient, immediate, and ultimately unsatisfying. Life's purpose is not found.

It may be that some of us change our true identity to create a perception of who we are even though we ultimately know our God given truth. It is possible to shed this mask through maturity and the recognition that we cannot invent someone better than God's intention for us. Then we can do the work required of our divine life. Once we are cognizant of the Light, it will direct us.

In finding our soul, we displace the ego. The ego is our ally until it becomes critical of God's creation. Then the spirit, which has slowly been preparing, is called upon to stop our constant ego satisfaction.

The spirit sees us as the loving potential that exceeds the confines of our human body. We are the eternal light that does not require materialism. Because we find our divinity in the presence of our human body, the ego forever challenges our spiritual growth like a jealous lover. IHood will continue its struggle to juggle the human and divine elements of our existence, while the spirit waits patiently for us to choose love, quietly undermining egoic longing, until we no longer have a mortal existence. Then we will have a sense of accomplishment and wisdom to stay on our purpose until our body ends and our spirit continues to be. Someone once told me, "It matters not if you gain success in your life; it matters that you live in a way that you deserve it."

Middle Age

In our society, middle age is considered the time to "retire" from our work. It has many different meanings for those in this stage of life. If the work has been unfulfilling and a grind, it can be a moment to rejoice. Others of us who were more fortunate to find complete satisfaction in our daily work routine find a vacant hole is left at retirement. Some of us never "retire." We continue doing what we always have, hoping to delay physical limitations. Retirement is intended to refer to our work, not to our entire existence. Our productivity as a spiritual human being must continue in spite of leaving our work.

Under further consideration, total retirement can be perceived as an insult to our spiritual existence. How can we spend an entire lifetime gathering skills, honing our intellect, experiencing a life that is unique to our purpose, and then just walk away? We can leave our job, but not our productivity.

Just because our bodies reach a certain age, it is not the trigger to return to an egocentric mindset we started abandoning as teenagers. Middle age is a time to give the fruits of our purposeful journey to another, not a regressive return to self. This is not a time to begin rewarding ourselves. Do we only look at our jobs for ego identity? The reward for life's journey is not found on this earth; it is found beyond our bodies, in the spiritual light that guided us to our purpose. Our reward was given to us at birth, when our bodies joined our spirits. The gift of life was given so that we could complete a powerful assignment given to us by our Creator. We must not squander our gifts with the mistaken notion of retirement merely prompted by an age indicator.

Over the years I have seen middle-aged retired people filling their days with pleasure seeking, alcohol, and television. What is the merit of this behavior? It is no wonder we witness retirees losing their way, turning back into the fool, becoming depressed because the reward is not satisfying. Life becomes meaningless.

The middle age years, especially in this century, offer a variety of opportunities. It gives us time to tweak, retool, and recharge our skill bank, to do any number of continued learning that could add to the uniqueness of who we are and what we have become. It is the time to read more books, take classes in oil painting, sculpture, welding, and other pastimes we didn't have the time for when we were younger. It isn't a coincidence, because God is still guiding us toward our best, most ultimate maturity. We still have much to offer. This is not the time to become takers again. We are still setting an example for our children, and now our grandchildren. We have more hills to climb; more love to give, and more spirituality to spread. It is a time to continue on our path of giving ourselves for the sake of others.

Reader Reflections

12
Spiritual Evolvement

Advanced Age: Wisdom and Reflection

IN A PERFECT WORLD, when we reach advanced age we are fully mature with the worldly experiences to have successfully found our spiritual path. Many lucky enough to have gained this level of evolvement are likely to be living spiritually exemplary lives and are instruments of love on a daily basis. However, because we are spirits in a human body, it is more likely than not that we fall somewhere between this optimum and "I still have no idea why I'm here." We are a work in progress.

This is the time we should look back and evaluate our life's work. We judge ourselves, rightly or wrongly, on the merits of our accomplishments. We have regrets for that which is unfinished or imperfect. We argue, assess, compare with others, defend, and rate our worth; much as we did when we were teens. But we don't have a lifetime to right the wrongs now. Most of us come up short in our self-evaluations. We are disappointed in our accomplishments. We wonder what happened to our dreams. We wonder why we are less valued than we hoped.

So what do we do? We go about the task of accepting who we

are and where we have gone, and continue to find our way into our life's purpose. If we are wise, we recognize that we have the potential to be game changers until we take our last breath. We see ourselves as late bloomers and go about living the quality life we deserve and owe to our loved ones with productive, fruitful, "other centered" living.

In a wonderful book by Joan Anderson, *A Walk on the Beach,*[13] the author reflects on conversations with her mentor, Joan Erikson. Ms. Erikson was the wife and collaborator to Erik Erikson, whose work is essential to this book and understanding one's IHood. Ms. Erikson was in the unenviable position of placing her husband in a nursing home during his advanced years. At this stage, he did not recognize her, nor was he able to complete basic tasks required for independent living.

The deterioration of our body is the bane of our physical existence and the last physical experience during our earthly stay. Ms. Anderson discusses the difficulty in accepting the inevitability of this final stage of life: "No matter how you look at it, old age is more negative than positive." Joan said that she thought putting an elder in a nursing home was a bit like taking the person to the dump. "The facilities are usually so far out of town, and the poor inmates are estranged from everything real about life." Ms. Erikson also cites "Old age demands that we garner and lean on all previous experience," and "Having practiced my whole life to be independent, I have these virtues to lean on now." She didn't want to admit it to herself, but she felt this stage was more difficult than the others.

Erikson isn't atypical in her concern for nursing homes. They do not reflect the quality of life we want for our advanced years.

---

13 Broadway Books, 2004

Concern becomes prominent in conversations had by those approaching old age, perhaps because the inevitable demise of our physical presence is obvious and death is nipping at our heels. Mentally, we are not finished with life; yet we squeeze out every bit of potential from the human system while we can. We race against time.

In *Old Age 1: A Conversation with Joan Erikson at 90*[14] she said, "Wisdom and integrity are something that other people may see in an old person, but it's not what this old person is feeling. That's what kind of roused me up to see what it was that old people do feel, and what they have to face." Ms. Erikson stated that she and her husband originally formulated this theory during their middle years during a time when she romanticized this stage but once she was in it herself, she experienced a host of problems, including forgetfulness, physical limitations, and facing the certainty of death.

The feeling of well-being heavily influences the way elderly people view their circumstance. As long as good health is present, the vital force of spirit seems to persist easily. We appreciate that we have our imprint, our purpose, and we continue to share what we have until God pulls the plug. Once we are infirmed, or unable to live a life of quality, it seems less and less likely that we can influence our independent expression of purpose. Indeed, our purpose may then change. We may transcend into nothing more than a reminder to those who still are functional that time on earth is limited; in fact, it runs out. The lesson is that we need to use our time wisely and be instruments of love in any way possible. The spiritual DNA is still within us, pushing its strength into our frail existence, to make our goal, to assure we put into place the puzzle

14 Davidson Films, Inc. 1993

piece; we weave the fabric of the quilt that is ours to complete in our mission. We don't know when our value is over, our creation complete. We will only know when our physical presence on this earth is no longer needed. We will then be finished, and God will release our spirit for its return to His heavenly embrace. We will be home, knowing our journey is complete.

Advanced age is the time to complete our promises. We learn to accept our circumstances as they are, taking the opportunity to transform other's lives through the example of love and perseverance. Until we reach this final stage, we can offer transportation to the elderly no longer able to drive, pick up groceries for those too ill to go to the store, and provide conversation to the lonely. Use your imagination; imagine what you would need at that stage. We can volunteer in children's hospitals where we take a dog on a leash for a touch of love; we can work in a food pantry, organize grandparent days, counsel entrepreneurs or teach a class at a community college. We can become a buddy for the disabled or the fatherless. The list is endless.

The questions may be raised: "Do I never get to golf again? Is it bad to play cards with my friends?" Obviously, God doesn't expect us to become indentured servants in our life's purpose. But in our prolonged life span we need to recognize the need to change our present misguided thinking, because a life is supposed to be productive and spiritually centered, not ego centered and self-absorbed. It is only in the demonstration of love and caring; expressing commitment to our fellow humans, when we will find satisfaction and joy in our advanced age.

Just as the new car did not bring anything but momentary happiness, so it is with empty hours of unproductive time and moments of misspent spiritual potential. We reject those activities that lead to depression and despair; we choose our aesthetic work;

our giving of love; the fulfillment of other needs. Ultimately, this will refill us once again in an unending cycle of our true meaning. This is why we are here.

We don't have to look very far to find examples of those who have succeeded in their life purpose: Thomas Edison put his own life in jeopardy when he saved a three year old boy from being hit by a train (not to mention inventing the light bulb). Mother Teresa, who knew at an early age she had a calling to serve her fellow man, "followed Christ into the slums of Calcutta to serve him among the poorest of poor." Anna Mary Robertson, also known as Grandma Moses, used her talents as an artist when she could no longer complete farm tasks because of arthritis. Her primitive style presents a powerful view of life, depicting no unhappiness or aging. Nelson Mandela resisted the National Party's apartheid policies as a young lawyer in Africa. Twenty years later, he was arrested for his views and sentenced to hard labor. He was imprisoned at Rot Prison, off Cape Town. He consistently refused to compromise his position to gain freedom. His beliefs triumphed when he was released nearly thirty years later. These people were not defined by the amount of money they accumulated, but by the contribution they made to God's work and creation.

13
IHood and Motivation

The Transition from Ego to Spirit Based Motivation

ABRAHAM MASLOW[15] IS AN expert I often quoted as a professor, preparing teachers to transform our world. I used to emphasize that motivation comes from within; we can inspire others; we can be the cheerleader to urge them on; but we can't force action, much like the old saying, "You can lead a horse to water, but you can't make it drink."

Motivation is the second piece in awakening to our spirit, while maturation is the first. They sweeten our human journey in life. They are the mortar and material that pave our road to full evolvement.

Physiological Motivation

Babies come with a huge needs package: first they need air for the breaths they take; then food, water and sleep; shelter to keep them warm; and constant nurturing. These needs are mostly physiologically based, an elemental level to existence, but a huge motivating force. They would die if these needs were not met. The

---

15   Abraham Maslow, *Motivation and Personality*, 1954

basic instinct for survival is a very strong element to existence; and is the beginning of our experience.

I have included physical touch and cuddling in this needs set, even though neither Maslow nor other behavioral scientists associated with motivational theory mention it. The reason I include this physical/emotional need is based upon conclusions from studies performed in European orphanages where high mortality rates were reported for infants who did not receive even minimal physical cuddling or touching.

Though the physiological level of motivation is associated with the beginning phase of life, it is important to realize that when we are threatened by the loss of satisfaction of these needs, we are motivated by the survival mode again. We are motivated to survive through hardships. The adult survivor, however, often offers prayers to God during these times. This is when our spirit can offer the support of hope to comfort those surviving a life dominated by stress.

Ego, despite negative implications, is actually needed for our acquisition of basic needs; it is a survival mechanism for our body. Ego pushes us to do more to satisfy needs. Since four of the five levels of needs that motivate us are needs of deficit, we automatically turn to our ego to fill them.

Only one level of need, the need for self-actualization, is based upon our spiritual growth, which is not seen as a deficit in human existence, but as an expansion of who we are intended to become. Self-actualization is the peak experience of our existence, the place where spirit flourishes. When we are fully motivated as humans, when we have fulfilled the needs our human life requires, we are prepared for motivation to the highest level of being. We must succeed at all the other "deficit" need motivated levels of existence to get there.

Safety Motivation

Once the basic physiological needs of our bodies are satisfied, we seek to satisfy needs for safety. These include personal security, financial security, wellness, and protection from adversity. Physical disasters and war continue to motivate us to seek out safety. Though much of our undeveloped world is at risk, there is evidence that societies still satisfy the need for self-protection and safety.

Depending on our circumstances, we might find ourselves oscillating between different need driven motivators. In an economic downturn, the need for financial security may be high on our needs list. Those of us who grew up in difficult times may find that prolonged financial hardship motivates our choices as we mature. It's common for those who have lived through recessions to seek a job with great security but low financial reward over one that provides great financial gain but is high risk. Our experience motivates us to hold on to what we have, and seek out what is safe.

We can see how these needs motivate us when safety is at stake. Hope (spirit) continues to play a major role with those who have matured and then find themselves again at this level of need satisfaction. Circumstances change, finding us moving into more primary need levels. When we reach higher levels of need, we can more easily make spiritually dominated choices, even in the face of one's security. Mother Teresa, for example, was physically at risk as she worked with the poor and sick in India. In her spiritual maturation, she saw her body as a tool to administer love and healing. She knew her purpose and lived it despite physical dangers. Mother Teresa, as she underwent her initial exposure to survival safety, may not have been sufficiently mature or motivated towards anything more than filling a deficit at the time it was presented.

Social Motivation

Since we are social beings, the next set of needs we encounter involves our urge to fulfill feelings of belonging. Typically, we are motivated by the search for identity within our own families first, and then expand our sights to other relationships and associated attachments. This need for belonging continues throughout life, manifested in communities, organizations, small and large groups, teams, gangs, and in the search for intimate partners, mentors, and colleagues. Ultimately, we form bonds we hope will lead to emotionally based relationships.

In *Join the Club*[16], Tina Rosenberg interestingly points out that a solution to poverty, disease, and alienation is rooted in peer pressure, a strong behavioral motivator that is human nature. This is a fascinating theory of how peer pressure can serve as the social cure. She presents an array of examples of how social problems are solved using clubs. One example from India was a program for rural, illiterate, abused, and poor women who trained as health workers. The results indicate that the club has been a change agent for these women, resulting in new roles through which to cope with their lives, as well as to find personal satisfaction from supportive colleagues, giving them status and hope.

The need for belonging may be so powerful that it can result in personal danger as well, however. Some are so motivated by the need that they join street gangs and take chances of being harmed or arrested, in order to fulfill expectations of other gang members. Their need for safety is overridden by the need for camaraderie and acceptance.

These very issues of placing ourselves at risk for the sake of such foolishness are why we again emphasize the *importance*

---

16 Rosenberg, 2011

of maturation to motivation. Maturity becomes very important when assessing our social situation, since those who are young and desperate for companionship often make poor decisions. We have read and seen stories about lonely teens retaliating against their school mates in futile attempts to "get even" for the hurt and disservice they feel were caused by rejection. Their reactions suggest adults could not prepare them to become adequately mature or satisfied with the levels of love and acceptance needed to function in their lives.

Motivation of Esteem

When we can take care of ourselves, we are ready to open up to sharing with others. Since we now should feel physiologically comfortable, environmentally safe, and socially stable, we are now motivated to gain esteem for what we have become thus far in our lives. Though this may well be a source of ego satisfaction, it is also possible to see a spiritual component manifested in our behavior.

Self-esteem is gained through our confidence, achievements, and respect for others and ourselves. It is also a time when we receive respect from others. Feeling respected gives us value. We feel that our accomplishments are noticed, that we are seeing a payoff for our efforts with the skills and talents that we have trained for during our life. Those who have not acquired what they deem to be a successful set of skills will experience low self-esteem. This is problematic since either the person has not acquired a skill level worthy of praise or he has not heard the amount of praise that he feels is deserved.

The bottom line is that each of us must be able to view our accomplishments by accepting and acknowledging them ourselves, first and foremost. If we don't believe in self, then no amount of praise and accolades will produce the esteem desired. Maslow noted that this need, the need to respect ourselves, is at a higher level than the need for respect from others, since it is a deal breaker in our aspiration for success. It is much more difficult to lose self-respect than the respect of others.

Psychological depression and imbalance may plague those who do not achieve esteem. Maslow felt that a fellow social scientist, Alfred Adler was right when he proposed[17] that low self-esteem and inferiority complexes were at the root of most psychological problems. I agree. If we find ourselves in this place, we may need psychological help to right our thinking.

Motivated to Self-Actualize Level V

Maslow calls this last level *growth motivation,* in contrast to *deficiency motivation,* since it doesn't involve balancing our needs or keeping them in a state of homeostasis. In fact, we become stronger at this level because we are "feeding" our needs. At this stage, the spirit demonstrably makes decisions that benefit others since we reach a level of highest motivation and undoubtedly reach maturity sufficient to serve others.

Though Maslow feels that this level is not reachable without complete homeostasis at the lower four levels, many researchers give multiple examples to the contrary. I believe that with sufficient maturity, we can overcome obstacles that could normally hinder our growth. Difficulties that demand resolution may arise, but we are able to find pragmatic solutions. Thus, we are not totally thwarted by threatening circumstances.

Certain personality traits are observed in those who have reached this level of motivation in their lives. They exhibit the ability to be reality centered and can differentiate between truth and fiction. They are problem centered, looking for solutions. They

---

17   *The Individual Psychology of Alfred Adler,* 1956

are happy to be alone and have few but good friendships, versus having shallow relationships. They can focus on problems outside themselves. The self-actualizers recognize they have all they need; they live independently. Social pressure does not affect them; they are nonconformists. Their humor is not hostile, using themselves as the target of human condition. They are not judgmental, preferring to "take you the way you are," while at the same time being highly motivated to change what they see as negative traits in themselves.

They have the ability to express "democratic values," and demonstrate humility in their dealings with others; they respect others and exhibit openness to their ethnicity. These people are quick to show appreciation and are creative as well. They are able to see the big picture in life, the meaning of who they are, and why they are here.

It would seem that these self-actualizers are perfect people. Maslow did note, however, that there were times when they displayed ruthlessness, surgical coldness, and loss of humor. Indeed, they are spirits in a human condition. We will always demonstrate our imperfection while on earth, while our spirit will always strive for the perfection in loving others.

Unfortunately, we see few self-actualized people in our world, as Maslow found in his research. People may not aspire to these values because their prior basic needs may not have been met. We are not bad people if we have not reached self-actualization. We hope to be motivated in this direction at some point in our lives. It is my belief that parents (and their parents), can change the number of those able to reach self-actualization by placing more emphasis on their outward, unconditional expression of love and showing a willingness to teach responsibility to children. Through patience and example, we can curtail the lingering habits of the ego, symptoms of our immaturity, and allow the spirit to prevail.

Reader Reflections

14
Following the Clouds
Living in Truth and Peace

WHEN I STARTED MY journey to write this inspired book, I questioned my energy to do the work required. I prayed to God for guidance. I knew I had a message to share, and knew there were people out there in search of it. It seemed though, to be a task for someone more youthful, with more energy. A friend of mine, who happens to be a Kabala teacher from California, told me that my story reminded her of Moses, who had a similar struggle. He was asked to lead his people out of enslavement when he was a very old man. I pointed out that I was no "Moses." She simply said, "God asks of us that which we are able to do. Just follow the clouds, Jill. Follow the clouds."

Age doesn't really matter in this life, nor does the magnitude of the task. It is answering the call to purpose. I now know my path; I believe I started preparing for it long ago. The knowledge I acquired in my profession has been invaluable in helping me explain the concept of IHood. My path is also bound in the living truth and in seeking peace through love, every day.

Our world is now in a critical period of evolution. There is great chaos, both physical and emotional. It seems the rules we live by are being made by our human ego, not our spirit; the material illusion looks increasingly tempting as we plummet in a spiral away from truth. Our children are being sacrificed in our quest for financial gain and the appearance of fulfillment. One has to question the compass we seem to be following. Is it leading us in the direction of earthly gain, or the unveiled truth of our purpose? It must be one or the other, since our ultimate purpose is to love and serve. It is fine to enjoy material comforts. It is only when we find we can't live without them that we witness the service to ego self.

What dominates our motivation? Are we living our truth through exercising integrity in our behavior? Are we choosing a faith built on convenience rather than conviction?

The Dalai Lama was asked, "What is the best religion?"

"It's the one that gets you closest to God. It is the one that makes you a better person." [18]

Again, he was asked, "What is it that makes me better?"

"Whatever makes you more compassionate, more sensible, more detached, more loving, more humanitarian, more responsible, and more ethical. The religion that will do that for you is the best religion. I am not interested about your religion or if you are religious. What really is important is your behavior in front of your peers, family, work, community and the world. Remember, the universe is the echo of our actions and our thoughts. If I act

---

18 www.dalailama.com

with goodness, I will receive goodness. If I act with evil, I will get evil. You will always have what you desire for others. Being happy is not a matter of destiny. It is a matter of options.

Take care of your thoughts because they become your words. Take care of your words because they become your actions. Take care of your actions because they become your habits. Take care of your habits because they will form your character. Take care of your character because it will form your destiny, and your destiny will be your life. There is no religion higher than the truth."

If we were religious people, it would seem that we might wonder about the best way to live our lives in order to follow our spirits. In *Wisdom of the Celtic Saints*,[19] it is quoted that Saint Brenden asked Ita (a sixth century abbess, who founded a monastery in County Limerick), "What were the most pleasing works to God and which were most displeasing?" Ita replied, "Three things that please God most are true faith in God with a pure heart, a simple life with a grateful spirit, and generosity inspired by charity. The three things that most displease God are a mouth that hates people, a heart harboring resentments, and confidence in wealth." Even if one were not religious, a person who has a belief in social morality would find these answers equally appropriate, since they appeal to integrity and the value of life.

When we follow the clouds in completing our journey on earth, it is important we live in truth and not chaos. Chaos is an

---

19   Sellner, 1993

obstacle to truth. Truth will not mislead, as it is fact. If we believe truth is different for everyone, we have created an illusion. This belief evolves from thinking there is a hierarchy of people: that some are better than others. Each proves their truth by attacking the other's values; justified by saying values differ. Those who hold different values then must be enemies. This allows for degrees of truth among illusionists.

Guilt is an obstacle to creating peace, created on earth by the ego. It links us to darkness, not to light. Ego rewards its followers with pain, because it convinces us the best in life is found in this world, not in our spirits. In ego, we lose our hope because there is only temporary fulfillment in what the ego offers. Guilt causes fear; we must learn to release it. In doing so, we allow love and light to shine upon us. There is no fear in love.

Truth and peace are found within. We were born into the world in a spiritual state. We can regain it by continuously seeking inside and not outside of ourselves. When we look outside of ourselves - to the world - we will never find our happiness: our truth and peace. We will only find pain because it is a fruitless search. Our insistence that happiness is elsewhere is futile. Our spirit holds the answer to who we truly are. An unveiling of our truth is our ultimate peace.

Do we have to reach a certain age to find our true self? No. In fact, many young people seem to know their direction in life almost from the beginning. Some, however, spend a lifetime of searching. They are rarely happy, and never fulfilled. This is not what our Lord had in mind when we were created. The temptations of the flesh are many; religious leaders have fallen and many of us have lost our way. Hope is seen in the new red car, not in helping the crying child. We are functioning in an unconscious world, seeking fulfillment from a menu that satisfies our bodies, rather than our souls. We search for temporary happiness in our culture of need, overlooking the glory of giving our love to each other. We must live in our true purpose and stop denying what has been gifted to us.

We are guided by divinity in the Holy Spirit; we continue to strive toward our goal of purpose, constantly being reminded that we are living in an egocentric body. Often we feel we are "neither here, nor there." We continue as best we can. There is a quote from Jonathan Swift's 1706 body of work *Thoughts on Various Subjects*[20]: "We have just enough religion to make us hate but not enough to make us love one another."

When we believe the world holds the answer to our happiness, we live in the ego, the body. We constantly wander, looking for that which can't be found. Believing only in what we are and what we are not. This searching implies we are not yet whole.

In December of 2009, I met a remarkable woman named Gloria in a hospital waiting room. We were both waiting for our husbands to have MRIs. Her husband had a brain tumor too. She told me she had gone crazy when she first found out, searching for the right doctors and the right treatment. They were waiting for the phone call to have him go for treatment. Everything was packed but the call never came. Appointments were canceled. She was desperate. Finally, she stopped trying to control everything and let go (or "let God," as Wayne Dyer often says). She said it was as if blinders were taken off her eyes. She went to a library to borrow a *Reader's Digest* because her own subscription had lapsed. There was a pile of outdated ones to take for free, and she took them. When she returned home with her husband, he tossed the copies on the kitchen counter. The top book immediately opened

---

20 Swift, *Thoughts on Various Subjects*, 1706

to an article about Doctor Spitzler, Barrows Neurological Institute in Phoenix, Arizona. "I knew it was God, and he had been there all the time", she said.

Gloria, like all of us, had forgotten to look inside to her spirit. She followed the lead of ego, determined that she would be able to find the answers that would help her husband. The good news was Gloria's husband went to that doctor in Arizona and had his procedures. He was well on the road to recovery. I'll never forget what she said before leaving the waiting room, encouraging me that all would be well with my husband. "Think about a cloudy day. It's gloomy. But above the cloud, the sun is always shining, even though we don't see it. Our life is the same; God is always there, but we don't always see Him."

My husband survived too.

Once in a while, I am lucky enough to have incredible insight pass on to me. The following was the result of such an event, documented in my journal in the early hours of May 31, 2011.

> Holy Spirit reveals to us the actions we must take to do God's work. Only if we are mature, or conscious of this, can we fulfill our mission. Each decision, large or small, that is made with the divine spirit within leads us closer to our purpose. It is in us, with us. We do the work of our creator while in this life. It is the divine message in all living things. Our DNA is naturally occurring. It is embedded in us. But if we do not resist the ego, we will fail in our greatest work: to love and serve others. Martin Luther King, Jr. said that love will save civilization. It is the hardest, most confusing toil we have at times but it is our supreme happiness when we recognize

that we are completing our assignment. We are by nature cooperative and competitive, and we would rather grow in the light of understanding the role of lovers of all on earth. All living things are to this purpose. We must survive, but we also must love in our survival. We do not make music when in our personal behavior we bring discomfort and unhappiness to others. When we take our guards away and openly love another just because we share the very air that we breathe, that is what is divine in us. God didn't parcel out the air for only the few, or water for one race or one class. God gave us all. We have distorted our mission; we have been sidetracked by false assumptions of personal gain and accomplishment. We are the hands of God, to reveal that there is a better way to live our lives. It is the intent to be the example to the young; the helpmate of contemporaries; the protector of all living things; the old, and feeble; those who are not able to help themselves. Desmond Tutu says, "God tells us, 'I don't have anybody else except you.'"[21] We each have the power of one: just do something.

It is not our purpose to further the actions of the unconscious or enable the lazy and weak of spirit. We are their teachers ... we need to raise them up to consciousness by example and challenge their direction in life ... we may not always be successful, but we must persevere ... in God's strength. If we

---

21 http://journalofsacredwork.typepad.com

begin to lose our own spirit in the process, then we must leave one and go to the next, for ego is a hard stake in one's heart. We must accept that we are not always able to conquer all that we see as the devil's work. Though, as one with God, we are duty bound to try. Perseverance can become an unconscious behavior, turning us to ego on the part of the helper. If a person is unwilling to walk in the light, he has the right to choose that. We can obsess in our efforts, seeing this as a "win" for God and us, but we cannot force our will any more than God would do so. Free will must be their course of action. We must step away. Just as we must stop a small child from destroying a living creature, we must turn our back on selfishness that persists, for there is no maturity in such action. It is defiling the purpose of others in their greater mission; time can be ill spent when treading water. If the unconscious is unwilling to change from self-focus to other focus, they are unwilling to take on mature responsibility and will continue to choose self over other as long as they do not have light shining on them to reveal their ignorance. We can point to their behaviors without judgment and hope that their enlightenment will lead them to reconsider their life's work. But we must not be unduly delayed in our journey by the actions of the unwilling, lest it keep us too long in one place.

As guardians of life, we prepare the young to live wisely and with regard to our use of talents and responsibility for self and others. Once of age, we no longer can impose more than they are willing to take by example. Their free choice is now their guardian. They must rely upon their truth. Just as an unwilling horse will not abide a rider, an adult may refuse his purpose as well. We must accept that which we can change, and leave the rest to God. Thanks be to God.

There will be a time when we will all stop our search; there will be a stillness of our mind, an unveiling of our truth, and ultimate peace. We will no longer feel a need to defend who we are, for truth needs no defense; no attack is possible. Truth will correct all errors in our mind of illusions and bring us peace. It will carry us in this world with the promise of changes that we are here to make. We will correct the errors that surround the world, as truth corrected the errors of our mind. We will be at peace. We will have found our purpose and we will be able to answer our eternal question, and we will know why we are here.

Reader Reflections

Appendix Table I

The following table represents various stages in life corresponded with the dominant influences between ego and spirit. The IHood continuum depicts input from both ego and spirit. While ego and divine spirit have a strong influence, our free will ultimately determines the choice we make when reaching a decision. Our IHood remembers the decision outcome, creating a body of experiences that influences future decisions. The left side of the continuum shows life stages that are heavily influenced by our ego. The right side of the continuum shows those stages heavily influenced by our divine spirit. The decisions we make are the balance between our ego and spirit, defined as our IHood. We aspire to evolve toward spiritually dominated decisions.

EGO DOMINATION	SPIRITUAL DOMINATION
* IHOOD IDENTITY	* ADVANCED AGE
* THE INTEGRATION OF HUMAN EGO AND DIVINE SPIRIT	
* A NON-STATIC RELATIONSHIP	
* IHOOD CONTINUUM	
* CHILDHOOD	

Decision Making

Human Ego ————————————————— Spirit Divine
Influence   Influence

Free Will

Choice Outcome Experiences

* Dominant Ego or Spirit Influence Depends Upon Maturation
Achieved © Dr. Jill Little

Afterword

As this book was being prepared for publication, Dr. Jill Little passed away. She was hospitalized from October 2011 until just before her death in early March 2012.

Jill was a brilliant woman. From her education and teaching background, to the love she carried for everyone she met. She did not consider physical appearance, wealth, or status; she considered only the souls/spirits and inner selves of people. Everyone who knew Jill is certain she is in heaven with God because of her exemplary life.

The people of this world will sorely miss her. Jill made a huge difference for many and left this earth a better place.

About the Author

"You were born into this world in a spiritual state with truth and peace within. It can be regained by searching 'inside', not 'outside' of ourselves. If we look outside ourselves, we will never find happiness; our truth and peace. We will only find pain because it is a fruitless search. Our insistence that happiness is elsewhere is futile, it is within each of us."

– Dr. Jill Little

Jill's relationship with faith and spirituality began when she was 7, when she was baptized in a small rustic Chapel on Panther Lake in Upstate NY. Following her baptism was a life-long dedication to learning about different faiths and the relationship between ego and spirituality.

Dr. Little was a teacher, philosopher, and student of life focused on serving as an instrument of love and peace wherever she went. She earned a B.S. in Elementary Education from Syracuse University, a M.Ed. from Temple University in Guidance Counseling, and a Ph.D. in School Administration from Syracuse University.

IHood: Our GPS for Living is Dr. Little's sixth book and her life's work. As we weave ourselves into the fabric of the world Jill believed in, we develop and access the innate abilities to love and serve each other. When our physical time in this world draws to a close, our contribution – a spiritual legacy – continues to integrate. Her belief, as felt throughout IHood, is that a divine opportunity to fill one's life with grace and purpose exists for everyone. It may lay dormant amidst worldly distractions, but begs to be awakened, interrupted, and brought to the forefront of living.

CPSIA information can be obtained at www.ICGtesting.com
Printed in the USA
BVOW070334250413

319049BV00003B/4/P